Rev. Dr. Bill Newman Ph. D

The author of this book has been a dear friend of mine for many years. The challenge that we have in life is that our fathers were Irish! If you could only see Al Watson before he came to Christ as a teenager and to see him now as a statesman for God is just God's pure grace. God has and is using him in a remarkable way to touch nations for the Lord. His passion is for evangelism and then turning decisions into disciples. The ministry that he serves with, "Walk Thru The Bible," has been used mightily in giving Believers a great grip of the panorama of the scriptures. In Al's new book "Identity" you will gain a greater view of the Good News of the Gospel and it's power to transform lives. You will learn so much more of the majesty of God and of His Son our Lord Jesus Christ. May God use this book mightily.   Bill Newman.

Rev. Dr. Bill Newman Ph. D is a distinguished Australian speaker. He regularly addresses audiences of thousands across Australia and around the world.

Neil Johnson
Host of Vision Christian Radio's 20Twenty Program

'Al Watson is one of Australia's most resilient, faithful leaders with a heart for God and his purposes. He has been my guest many times and is known for his clarity, as a reservoir of biblical wisdom. Al's latest book will be a valuable resource for aspiring and mature Christian servants of God, and for those wanting to understand what makes our 'Identity' in Christ so valuable.'

Neil Johnson - Head of News and Current Affairs, and author of 'Public Christians in a Secular Age.

Rev. Bob Thomas

"It's well pitched, proceeds logically, written clearly, reveals the enemy within. It's a worthy publication."

Rev. Bob Thomas, former Moderator General of the Presbyterian Church of Australia and Editor Emeritus of New Life.'

Rev. Dr Allan Meyer Careforce Lifekeys Community Resources Inc.

"I was given the opportunity to engage with this book at a most significant moment. A few months before writing this endorsement my heart was stirred for the eternal destiny of a friend.
It was this same concern that gave birth to this book. I have been greatly encouraged by its clarity and focus as I share my faith with my friends. I am certain that this book will be an encouragement to the faith and witness of everyone who reads it."

Peter Thomas
Former Director/Principal Capernwray Bible School Australia;
part-time pastor Bowral Baptist Church

I'm very happy to recommend Al Watson's book 'Identity'. Al has the capacity to capture the rich truths of scripture and present them in very straightforward and challenging ways. Most importantly he presents the transforming presence of Christ in the believer as essential to our true 'identity'. Al has been a regular guest lecturer at Capernwray Bible School and has always faithfully laid down the foundational truths of the Gospel and the Christian life. His 'Walk-Thru-the Bible' ministry, New Life leadership and missions' heart have clearly equipped him to impact others with his passion and insight. This reflects the man of God that he is.
Peter Thomas.

Al Watson

Identity

About the Author:

Al Watson is a respected Bible teacher, preacher, and communicator of the Gospel. He serves as the CEO of *Walk Thru the Bible Australia Inc.* and Managing Director of *New Life Magazine*. With over 37 years of pastoral experience as the teaching pastor of four churches, Al brings deep insight and clarity to the Scriptures.

He is also a seasoned Bible college lecturer, radio and YouTube broadcaster, and a committed mentor to pastors. Al's passion is to equip Christ-followers to become disciple-makers. He is the author of the *Systematic Theology 101* series and the *Believe* series. Mr Watson continues to teach and train across Australia and beyond.

He is married to Judith and has three adult Children and six grandchildren. Al lives in Victoria Australia.

Identity

Al Watson

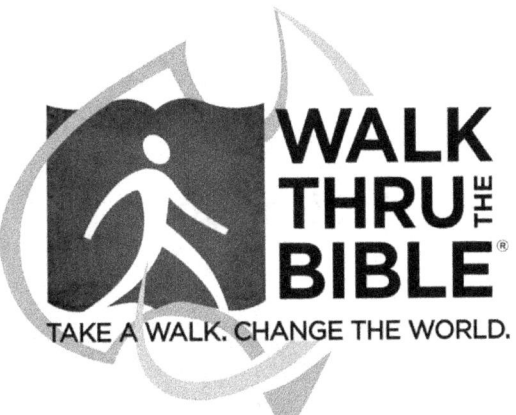

Walk Thru the Bible
Australia Inc.
P.O. Box 650
Dromana
Victoria 3936
Australia

info@walkthru.org.au

All scripture quotations are from the ESV unless otherwise indicated.

ISBN: 978-0-9941708-7-3

Book one in the "Believe Series" from John's Gospel

© Copyright. No part of this book can be reproduced without written permission from the owners.
©

Dedication.

To Judith,
my beloved wife, my helpmeet and partner in life for 55 years.
The faithful mother of our three children,
and the cherished grandmother of our six grandchildren.

Your love, strength, and steadfastness have been the quiet foundation of our family and the constant encouragement behind every page of this book.
With all my heart, I thank God for you.

INTRODUCTION:	8
CHAPTER ONE: 5 KEY CONCEPTS	10
CHAPTER TWO: 5 KEY CONCEPTS (PART 2)	27
CHAPTER THREE: JESUS THE WORD	48
CHAPTER FOUR: JESUS IS GOD	63
CHAPTER FIVE: JESUS THE CREATOR	75
CHAPTER SIX: JESUS THE LIFE	87
CHAPTER SEVEN: JESUS IS THE LIGHT	100
CHAPTER EIGHT: JESUS THE LAMB OF GOD	116
CHAPTER NINE: HIS NAME IS JESUS	126
CHAPTER TEN: JESUS THE TEACHER	140
CHAPTER ELEVEN: JESUS THE MESSIAH	157
CHAPTER TWELVE : JESUS THE SON OF GOD	172
CHAPTER THIRTEEN: JESUS THE KING OF ISRAEL	184
CHAPTER FOURTEEN: JESUS THE SON OF MAN	193
CHAPTER FIFTEEN: THE WINE AND THE BLOOD	209

Identity
CHAPTER SIXTEEN: THE TEMPLE AND THE RESURRECTION 225

Al Watson

Introduction:

With my wife being a singer, I have always had music in my world. There was one song that imprinted itself on my soul and has never left me. It was the Bill and Gloria Gaither song, "There's Just Something About That Name." Listening to a performance of it by the Gaither Quartet on YouTube, I noticed that Gloria added words not found in the original song, taking it to a different level. You will find a blend of her words in what follows.

Throughout history, emperors have tried to destroy it.

Philosophers have attempted to stamp it out.

Tyrants have spilled the blood of those who claimed it, hoping to erase its very existence.

Yet, it still stands. No force of man, no ideology, no act of violence has been able to silence its truth.

At the heart of "Identity" lies a name-one that has stirred nations, defied kingdoms, and transformed lives. A name spoken by angels, foretold by prophets, and declared with power: "Jesus."

The world has tried to redefine His identity in countless ways, but there is one identity that remains unshaken —the identity found in Him.

"One day, when time has run its course, every voice that has ever spoken, every soul that has ever lived, will join in one mighty chorus. On that day, every knee will bow, and every tongue will confess that Jesus Christ is Lord, to the glory of God the Father.

This truth cannot be undone, for it was not by chance that an angel appeared to a humble virgin and declared, "His name shall be called Jesus."

There is something about that name-something that defines, restores, and gives purpose. In a world searching for meaning, this book on His "Identity" calls us back to the one true identity that will stand for eternity.

Welcome to the journey.

Al Watson

Chapter One: 5 Key Concepts

There have been years of contemplation in writing this book, which I have called *Identity*. The genesis started when I was asked to come and speak at a retreat for young people who were voluntary counsellors at a Christian camp. The thought process started by asking the question,

"Where in the Bible does it outline what a person has to believe to be part of God's forever family?"

John 20:30-31 came to mind, for it appears that John intended his gospel to enable people to know what people must believe to receive life, and throughout his gospel the word *life* was understood to mean eternal life:

"Now Jesus did many other signs in the presence of the disciples, which are not written in this book; but these are written so that you may believe that Jesus is the Christ, the Son of God, and that by believing you may have life in his name."

Then I remembered John 3:36 defines the meaning of *life* even better:

"Whoever believes in the Son has eternal life; whoever does not obey the Son shall not see life, but the wrath of God remains on him."

Over the years, we have seen many changes in the way Christians have sought to present the Christian message. There is no doubt that Dr. Billy Graham's evangelistic crusades had a huge impact in Australia. In 1959, more than 130,000 people (almost 2% of the Australian population at that time) made a commitment to Christ. Historian Stewart Piggin uses the Australian Bureau of Statistics figures to show a drop in alcohol consumption, extra-marital births, and crime statistics following that time.

Identity

During the 1970s, 1980s, and 1990s, ministries such as Navigators, Student Life, Campus Crusade for Christ, Youth With A Mission (YWAM), ISCF, Young Life, and many others actively brought the gospel to students in universities and high schools. Many of these ministries continue to engage young people today. However, they are not as visible on campuses across the country as they once were, and we hear less about their impact. This decline is undoubtedly influenced by the significant shift in societal attitudes toward Christianity.

So, it's fair to ask: Has the Christian community lost faith in the message of the Gospel? Or is the Gospel still relevant in today's world? Some argue that few pastors today preach the true Gospel, instead offering a message that is centred on human needs and desires. The focus has shifted to what Christianity can provide to enhance one's personal life—things like peace, purpose, friendships, community, and camaraderie. The late evangelical theologian J.I. Packer echoed this concern, writing, "The subject of the old gospel was God and his ways with men; the subject of the new is man and the help God gives him. There is a world of difference. The whole perspective and emphasis of gospel preaching has changed."

This change can be seen in two extremes within Christian churches today. The first is complete heresy, and the second is what I call synthetic faith.

The following article was written by Rev. Dr. Lorraine Parkinson, Vice-President of the Progressive Christian Network of Victoria. The article, *"Why is Christianity Evolving?"*, was published in *Cross Light Magazine* in October 2013.

"Evolving Christianity is recognition of change already taking place in the church. There is a healthy doubt concerning the validity of fourth-century doctrines about God and Jesus for today's church. It frequently expresses concern about what we mean when we say 'God.' We do not believe in a male god 'up there' or 'out there' with Jesus Christ beside him waiting to return to earth. We have grown up in our faith and no longer believe in being saved from hell by a saviour Christ.

Al Watson

The church is the people. The evolving church is people whose idea of God has changed out of sight from the way they imagined God a decade or three ago. The evolving church is people who find the Christian Triune God of exclusivist dogma unhelpful. The evolving church is people uniting their scientific and philosophical knowledge of the world with their faith in God. It is people who look to the scripture as sacred wisdom for life but whose education has equipped them to notice the Bible's limitations. The evolving church is people who want to hear when a biblical story is just that—stories; including the narratives of Easter and Christmas."

Another message presents the Gospel as a means to enhance one's life, with the underlying question being, *"What's in it for me?"* This version of the Gospel focuses on the personal benefits of faith—promising experiences that will enrich one's life. As J.I. Packer described, *"this is a man-centred message, shifting the focus from God's work and purpose to what individuals can gain from faith."*

To others, the Gospel is treated as a formula—an intellectual agreement with certain biblical truths, followed by the recitation of a set prayer of dedication. This act is seen as the entry point into the family of God. I don't doubt that for many, this genuinely expressed their heart's desire and understanding of the Gospel, leading to a true spiritual transformation. However, for others, it may have been merely a process they tried—something that seemed reasonable at the time, influenced by those around them, but lacking deep personal conviction.

We, like many, still believe what Paul wrote in Romans 1:16-17:

"For the gospel is the power of God for salvation to everyone who believes, to both Jews and Greeks. For in it the righteousness of God is revealed from faith for faith, as it is written, 'The righteous shall live by faith.'"

I began reading and rereading the Gospel of John, seeking to understand its core message. If this book was written to explain the Gospel that saves, what exactly was its message? And to whom was it written? Was it intended as a training manual for Christ-followers, or was it meant to function as a gospel tract for unbelievers?

Identity

After careful consideration, I concluded that it serves both purposes. The following is the testimony of the Anglican Arch-Bishop of Sydney, and you will see how the Gospel of John was the way God brought him to faith.

Kanishka Raffel was born in London to Sri Lankan parents and was raised as a Buddhist. While studying law at Sydney University a friend gave him a copy of The Gospel according to John and he subsequently became a Christian.

Kanishka recounts his conversion as follows:

"I was raised in a loving home, and my mother nurtured me in Buddhism. In my third year at university, I devoted a year to studying the faith of my childhood. Subsequently, I had a conversation with a Christian friend, during which he told me that being a Christian meant he had given control of his life to Jesus. It was an answer that surprised me, to say the least! He offered me Mark's Gospel and John's Gospel to read, and I accepted. The Lord saved me as I read John's gospel some weeks later. In God's kindness, I saw that in response to Jesus' words and deeds, 'people were divided'. It made me consider why I was 'against' Jesus. Eventually, I realised I had no reason to oppose Jesus, and in some way that wasn't altogether clear to me, he was for me. John 6:44-45 ("No one can come to me unless the Father who sent me draws him. And I will raise him up on the last day. It is written in the Prophets, 'And they will all be taught by God.' Everyone who has heard and learned from the Father comes to me") were important. I saw that life is not an endless cycle but has a 'last day', and I was convicted that God was drawing me to his Son. So I came."

However, I believe its primary aim is to equip Christians with a deeper understanding of the truths and implications of the Gospel. The first thing we notice is that there seemed to be a clear division. Up to the middle of chapter 12, Jesus presented His message to the public, but in chapter 12, verse 36, John removes Jesus from public ministry by simply writing:

"When Jesus had said these things, he departed and hid himself from them."

For the rest of chapter 12, John gives us the reasons why people do not believe. Then from John chapter 13 onward, the ministry of Jesus was with the disciples, which ended at the end of chapter 17. Then we have all the events that led to His slaughter on the cross, His burial, and, after three days and nights in the grave, His resurrection.

The message of this Gospel is to reveal the true identity of Jesus, the Son of God, and to explain the meaning of the Gospel. Or, as Paul expressed it in Romans 1:2-4:

"The gospel of God, which he promised beforehand through his prophets in the holy Scriptures, concerning his Son, who was descended from David according to the flesh and was declared to be the Son of God in power according to the Spirit of holiness by his resurrection from the dead, Jesus Christ our Lord."

We mistakenly call it the Gospel of John. But does this Gospel provide good news— which is what the word *gospel* means—about John? No, it is the Gospel of Jesus Christ according to John. The same is true of the other three Gospels. They are the Gospels of Jesus Christ according to Matthew, Mark, and Luke.

Maybe we can start referring to this Gospel by its proper name: the Gospel or Good News about Jesus Christ, according to whichever Gospel writer you are reading from.

A Training Manual for Evangelism

My hope is that this book will serve as a training manual for evangelism, equipping believers to share the Gospel. We are all called to proclaim the Good News as we go—as Jesus commanded in the Great Commission:

Matthew 28:19

"In your going, make disciples..."

Identity

To help us understand "what is involved in sharing the Good News about Jesus", we must first grasp:

1. Who Jesus is—which is outlined in John chapter one.
2. What it means to believe in Him—which is also introduced in John chapter one.
3. How this life-transforming power is made possible—which is revealed in John chapter two.
4. From John 3 through John 11, we see how Jesus presented this Good News in various situations, engaging with different people in unique ways.

Jesus: The Light in the Darkness

It was John the Baptist that introduces Jesus to the world by uses the powerful metaphor of mental and spiritual darkness to describe the world in which people live. Into this darkness, he introduces Jesus as: "The true light, which gives light to everyone, was coming into the world." John 1:9. We will discover what part J.B. plays in bringing light to bear on Jesus later in our study. Those who embrace Jesus step out of darkness and into His marvellous light. They move from blindness to sight, darkness to light, and spiritual death to life in Him.

The 5 key steps:

"He was in the world, and the world was made through him, yet the world did not recognise him. He came to his own, and his own people did not receive him. Yet to all who did receive him, who believed in his name, he gave the right to become children of God, who were born, not of natural descent, nor of human decision, nor of the will of man, but of God." John 1:10-13.

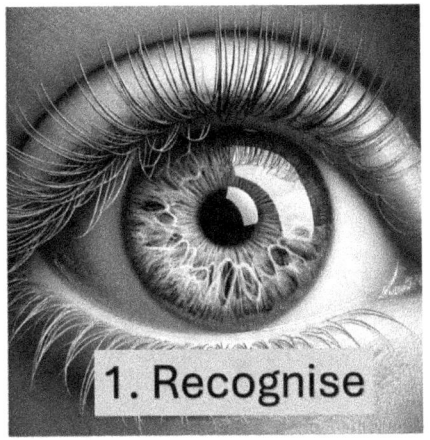

Within these four verses, we have the outline that will underpin the questions we use in our exploration of the first 12 chapters of John. We will also use 5 pictures that will become memory triggers, causing us to constantly keep our investigation on tract.

The pictures and the words are as follows:

The first is RECOGNISE. As verse 10 points out, when Jesus came to this world, the world did not recognise Him. But they should have, so that gives us a starting point for understanding where our evangelism should begin.

People need to RECOGNISE WHO JESUS IS. This is also what Hebrews 11:6 says, "And without faith it is impossible to please God, because *anyone who comes to him must believe that he exists* and that he rewards those who earnestly seek him."

So, we use the human eye to become our memory trigger making sure we start with seeking to take people to discover Jesus.

Jesus makes bold and profound claims about Himself, which we will examine in the next chapters. For now, the key point to emphasis is that to truly follow Jesus, we must personally affirm and accept all that He says about Himself. Unfortunately, many create a distorted version of Jesus—one that suits their own preferences rather than the Jesus revealed in Scripture.

We often wonder why people struggle to embrace the biblical revelation of His identity, especially when history provides overwhelming evidence for His existence. Clearly, the issue is not a lack of evidence. Instead, as Jesus Himself pointed out, the real obstacle is *the human will*.

People resist the true Jesus because acknowledging Him as the Gospels present Him carries profound implications—it demands something of them. Jesus addressed this in John 7:17, *"If anyone's will is to do God's will, he will know whether the teaching is from God or whether I am speaking on my own authority."* If you are willing you can know. Therefore this statement underscores that a willingness to submit to God is the key to recognising the truth of Jesus' words.

We often hear people speak about the *battle of the will*, and that is precisely what we see here. The issue is not that we *cannot* understand the facts presented—it's that we *don't want to*.

Some rationalise this resistance as part of a generational mindset. For example, Generation Z, as they are often called, tends to reject the idea of absolute truth, instead claiming that everyone can have their own version of truth. However, the reality remains—absolute truths do exist. The real question is not whether they exist, but whether we choose to accept them. Rejecting a truth does not make it disappear.

At its core, this is a spiritual battle. We will explore this conflict in greater depth when we examine Jesus as *Light* in a later chapter. As we do, keep in mind that a significant portion of our society has little to no knowledge of who Jesus truly is or what He has done on their behalf. This becomes especially clear in John's introduction to Jesus, where he uses twelve different names or titles to reveal His identity. These descriptions will help us discover a bigger and more accurate picture to the identity of Jesus.

How much does a person need to know before becoming a follower of Jesus? This is a good question. It would appear that the thief on the cross had no idea about Jesus, but Jesus said that "This day you will be with me in paradise". Nevertheless, the better we know a person, the more we trust that person. And we as evangelists will be better equipped the more we know about the identity of our Saviour. It is vital that people RECOGNISE WHO JESUS IS.

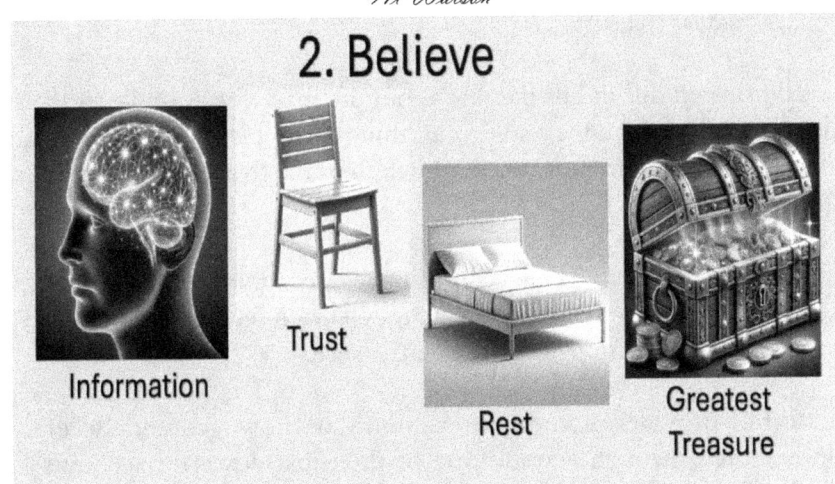

2. Believe

The second word and picture is, BELIEVE:

John calls us to believe in Jesus in John 1:12:

"But to all who did receive him, who believed in his name, he gave the right to become **children of God."**

This call to believe is the central message of the Gospel throughout the New Testament. Paul echoed this in Acts 16:31 when he told the Philippian jailer, *"Believe on the Lord Jesus Christ, and you will be saved."*

But what does it truly mean to *believe*? John uses this word 98 times in his Gospel, emphasising its importance. In the New Testament, the concept of belief involves four key elements:

- **Knowledge – It begins with the mind, where we understand the truth about Jesus.** This is the information we need to know.
- **Trust** – Belief moves beyond knowledge to trust, much like trusting a chair to hold your weight when you sit down.
- **Rest** – True belief brings a deep sense of peace, a state of being fully at ease, just as one feels when lying in bed and falling asleep.

- **Treasure** – Finally, belief in Jesus means that He becomes our greatest treasure.

Jesus illustrated this in His parable about the man who found a treasure hidden in a field. The man sold everything he owned—not because he wanted to own a farm, but because he desired the treasure buried within it (Matthew 13:44).

Similarly, when we truly believe in Jesus, we recognise that He is worth more than anything else. We are willing to surrender whatever He asks, because knowing Him is the ultimate treasure.

The Bible provides numerous examples of how genuine belief is demonstrated through action. One of the most powerful accounts is found in Daniel 3, where three young men—Shadrach, Meshach, and Abednego—displayed unwavering faith in God.

When commanded to bow before the golden image of Nebuchadnezzar, king of Babylon, they refused, knowing that God had strictly forbidden such worship in the Second Commandment. In his fury, Nebuchadnezzar ordered them to be thrown into a fiery furnace—so intense that it killed the soldiers who carried out the execution. Yet, to the king's astonishment, the three men were unharmed, walking freely in the fire. Even more remarkably, a fourth figure appeared alongside them, whom Nebuchadnezzar described as looking like *"a son of the gods."*

When the men emerged unscathed, the king declared:

"Blessed be the God of Shadrach, Meshach, and Abednego, who has sent his angel and delivered his servants, who trusted in him and set aside the king's command and yielded up their bodies rather than serve and worship any god except their own God." (Daniel 3:28).

These three men exemplify what it means to *treasure* God above all else. Their faith led to their miraculous preservation, but even if it hadn't, they were determined not to compromise. True faith is not contingent on favourable outcomes—it remains steadfast regardless of the cost. We only live like that when Jesus is our greatest treasure.

Being rescued from physical danger was not always the result for believers. Hebrews 11:35-40 recounts the suffering of others who remained faithful:

"Others suffered mocking and flogging, and even chains and imprisonment. They were stoned, they were sawn in two, they were killed with the sword. They went about in skins of sheep and goats, destitute, afflicted, mistreated—of whom the world was not worthy—wandering about in deserts and mountains, and in dens and caves of the earth."

This passage reminds us that faith does not guarantee earthly safety, but it does guarantee something far greater—eternal security in Christ.

Paul captures this reality in Romans 8:39, assuring us that *nothing*—not even death—can separate us from the love of God in Christ Jesus. With this saving faith, we walk through life with humility and trust, knowing that our hope is not confined to this world. As eternal beings, we hold to Paul's words in 2 Corinthians 5:8:

"To be absent from the body is to be present with the Lord."

True faith transcends our temporary existence and anchors us in the eternal promises of God.

Identity

3. Embrace

1. The third word is EMBRACE.

While John uses the word receive, and we indeed receive Christ when we believe, many misunderstand this as something purely physical— as if it requires an external action.

For example, when we eat bread or drink water, we take something tangible into our bodies. This makes it easy to assume that receiving Christ also involves a specific outward action. The emphasis then shifts to *doing*, as if there were a formula to follow.

When asked how they know they are Christians, many people point to a moment—a prayer they prayed, a baptism, or a confirmation ceremony. For them, a ritual marked the moment they *received* Christ. But is that what the Bible teaches?

When we examine biblical examples of conversion, we see that it often happened unseen, yet its effects became clearly visible later. Jesus Himself compared it to the wind in John 3:8:

"The wind blows where it wishes, and you hear its sound, but you do not know where it comes from or where it goes. So, it is with everyone who is born of the Spirit."

Just as we cannot see the wind but can observe its effects, true conversion is a work of the Holy Spirit—an inward transformation that is later evidenced in a changed life.

There must be a mental and heart-level embrace of Jesus. While a prayer can serve as a physical expression of that inward commitment, new life in Christ is ultimately a work of God. He breathes life into what was once a dead spirit, making us spiritually alive.

As we read through the Gospel of John, we see that the words "believe" and "receive" are often used interchangeably. For example, in John 1:12:

"But to all who did receive Him, who believed in His name, He gave the right to become children of God."

This is not describing two separate actions—it is one reality expressed in two ways. Believing is receiving, and receiving happens through believing. They are the same thing.

Paul's experience in Thessalonica further illustrates this truth. When he preached the Gospel there, some embraced Christ. He later explained what had taken place:

"And we also thank God constantly for this, that when you received the word of God, which you heard from us, you accepted it not as the word of men but as what it really is, the word of God, which is at work in you believers." (1 Thessalonians 2:13)

Breaking this down:

- The people *heard* the Gospel from Paul ("which you heard from us").
- They *accepted* it—not merely as human words but as divine truth ("not as the word of men but as what it really is, the word of God").
- The Word was then at work in them—they had *received* and *believed*, showing that true faith is a gift from God that transforms the believer.

This passage highlights the seamless connection between believing and receiving. Faith is not just an intellectual agreement; it is a life-changing response to God's truth.

The message that people heard, understood, and embraced was centred on Jesus—His teachings, His death, burial, and resurrection. This was

Identity

not just intellectual knowledge but a deep, personal acceptance of the truth about Christ.

Embracing Jesus—believing in Him—opens the door to true spirituality. This saving faith comes through hearing the Word of God (Romans 10:17). When a person embraces and trusts this message, the Holy Spirit gives new life to what was once spiritually dead, for Scripture tells us that we are all born spiritually dead (Ephesians 2:1). But once we believe, God makes His home within us.

From that moment, God is actively at work within believers, doing two things:

1. Giving new desires—a longing for righteousness and a heart that seeks after God.

2. Providing new abilities—empowering believers to live according to these new desires. As Philippians 2:13 states: *"For it is God who works in you, both to will and to work for His good pleasure."*

Paul further explains this transformation in Ephesians 1:13-14:

"In Him you also, when you heard the word of truth, the gospel of your salvation, and believed in Him, were sealed with the promised Holy Spirit, who is the guarantee of our inheritance until we acquire possession of it, to the praise of His glory."

The sealing of the Holy Spirit is a powerful concept. It is like an engagement ring, signifying that we are set apart for Christ—just as an engaged person is set apart for their future spouse. The Holy Spirit dwelling in us is God's pledge, His guarantee, that we belong to Him and that our inheritance in eternity is secure.

When we truly believe and embrace Jesus, we BECOME—we are transformed from the inside out, given new life, new purpose, and a new identity in Christ.

Al Watson

Here are **10 discussion and reflection questions** based on chapter 1.

Identity: Gospel Foundations:

1. What must a person believe to become part of "God's forever family," according to John 20:30–31 and John 3:36?

    - How does this compare with what is often presented in modern evangelism?

2. How has the presentation of the Gospel changed in recent decades, and what impact do you think this has had on both the church and society?

    - Use examples such as Billy Graham's crusades vs. today's approaches.

3. J.I. Packer contrasts the "old gospel" and the "new gospel." In your own words, what is the key difference between the two, and why does it matter?

4. What does Rev. Dr. Lorraine Parkinson's quote on "evolving Christianity" reveal about the challenges facing the modern church?

    - Do you think this evolution is helpful or harmful to the Christian message?

5. The Gospel of John is referred to as both a gospel tract for unbelievers and a training manual for believers. Which purpose do you think stands out most, and why?

6. Why do people struggle to recognise the true identity of Jesus, even when historical and biblical evidence is strong?

    - Reflect on Jesus' words in John 7:17.

Identity

7. What are the four elements of true belief in Jesus mentioned in the lecture?

    o   How do these elements go beyond just intellectual agreement?

8. The illustration of Shadrach, Meshach, and Abednego was used to demonstrate "treasuring" God. What does their story teach us about the cost and character of genuine faith?

9. What is the difference between externally "receiving" Christ (e.g., a prayer or ceremony) and the inward transformation that Scripture describes?

    o   How does John 1:12 clarify this?

10. The sealing of the Holy Spirit is described as a "guarantee" and compared to an engagement ring. How does this image shape your understanding of your relationship with God and your eternal security in Him?

Al Watson

Chapter Two: 5 Key Concepts (part 2)

1. We BECOME CHILDREN OF GOD:

"But to all who did receive him, who believed in his name, he gave the right to become children of God,…" 1:12.

Become is the key word here. A helpful way to understand what it means to become a child of God is by looking at the transformation of a grub into a butterfly. Inside the cocoon, something remarkable happens—a complete metamorphosis takes place.

The insect passes through four distinct phases, ultimately emerging as an adult that looks nothing like the larva it once was.

Spiritual Metamorphosis

In the same way, believers undergo a spiritual metamorphosis when they are born of God into His family. Before this, our spirit was dead, but through faith in Christ, it is resurrected to life. This transformation is so radical that Scripture describes us as becoming a completely new person—a new creation: *"Therefore, if anyone is in Christ, he is a new creation. The old has passed away; behold, the new has come."* (2 Corinthians 5:17)

However, just as a newborn must grow and develop, so must this new life in Christ mature. Spiritual growth is essential.

The apostle Peter urges believers to nurture their faith:

"Like newborn infants, long for the pure spiritual milk, so that by it you may grow up into salvation." (1 Peter 2:2) The "milk" Peter speaks of is the Word of God—the Bible. Growth after spiritual birth is crucial for a strong and thriving Christian life.

Paul echoes this concern when addressing the Christians in Corinth:

"Brothers and sisters, I could not address you as people who live by the Spirit but as people who are still worldly—mere infants in Christ. I gave you milk, not solid food, for you were not yet ready for it. Indeed, you are still not ready." (1 Corinthians 3:1-2)

The Call to Maturity

Just as a butterfly must struggle to emerge from its cocoon, so must believers actively pursue growth. Being born again is just the beginning—the goal is to mature in faith, deepening our understanding and commitment to Christ. This is why it is critical that, once born into the family of God, we take intentional steps to grow up into our faith.

Three Ways That Spiritual Birth Does Not Occur

As John continues, he presents three ways in which this new birth does not happen. These are common misunderstandings that can lead people to believe they are part of God's family when, in reality, they have not yet been born again.

1. *Not by Blood – Spiritual Birth is Not Inherited*

John first states that those who are born of God are *"not born by blood"* (John 1:13). This means that spiritual birth is not inherited. Just because someone's parents are Christians does not make them a believer.

There is always a danger that a person can learn the language of faith, observe Christian practices, and attend church, believing that these

Identity

outward actions make them part of God's family. But faith is not inherited—each person must be born again through personal faith in Christ.

This was precisely the case with Nicodemus, a deeply religious man who knew the Scriptures but was still outside the Kingdom of God. Jesus told him plainly:

"Unless one is born again, he cannot see the kingdom of God." (John 3:3)

> 2. *Not by the Will of the Flesh – Spiritual Birth is Not Achieved Through Human Effort*

The second misunderstanding about salvation is that people can somehow earn acceptance with God through their own efforts.

John corrects this by stating that salvation is *"not of the will of the flesh"* (John 1:13), meaning that no amount of personal striving, good deeds, or religious discipline can bring about salvation.

Paul reinforces this truth in Titus 3:4-5

"But when the goodness and loving kindness of God our Saviour appeared, he saved us, not because of works done by us in righteousness, but according to his own mercy, by the washing of regeneration and renewal of the Holy Spirit,"

Salvation is entirely a work of God's grace—it is not something we deserve or can work for. Grace means being given something we do not deserve. Even the very faith to believe in Christ is a gift from God. Ephesians 2:8 *"For by grace you have been saved through faith. And this is not your own doing; it is the gift of God."*

> 3. *Not by the Will of Man – Spiritual Birth is Not Bestowed by Religious Leaders*

The third mistake people make is thinking that religious leaders—whether pastors, priests, bishops, or even the Pope—have the power to make someone a Christian through religious rituals.

John makes this clear: salvation is *"not by the will of man"* (John 1:13). No religious authority can declare a person saved by performing a ritual or granting a church title.

Some traditions teach that baptism is the means of entering the Christian faith, but while baptism is a powerful symbol of faith, it does not bring spiritual rebirth. True salvation comes only through faith in Jesus Christ.

When you look at the baptismal services within different denominations, many give the impression that it is through baptism that a person is saved. We will quote one. "In baptism the Holy Spirit conveys the benefits of Christ's redemption. These benefits are the same as those proclaimed by the gospel and received in faith. According to the New Testament, baptism gives forgiveness of sins, justification, new birth as one enters the kingdom of God, and many other promises."

This is saying that the act of baptising a person is the act that makes a person a born-again child of God. And this act is mostly performed on an infant, who plays no part in the decision. This means that the baptiser, by this act, is making the child a child of God. However, that contradicts what John, inspired by the Holy Spirit, was saying. *"nor by the will of man"*.

How Does a Person Become a Child of God?

John 1:12-13 gives the clear answer:

"He gave the right to become children of God, who were born... of God."

To understand this, consider a simple analogy: What role did you play in your own physical conception and birth? The answer is none. You had no part in bringing yourself into existence. The same is true of spiritual birth—it is entirely the work of God.

Born of God—Not by Human Effort

Just as physical life is initiated by parents, spiritual life is initiated by God. This is why John emphasises that becoming a child of God is not achieved by inheritance, effort, or religious ritual— but by God alone.

A person becomes a child of God through a supernatural act of God's grace, where He:

1. Gives new spiritual life (John 3:3, *"You must be born again"*).

2. Gives the gift of faith to believe in Christ (Ephesians 2:8, *"This is not your own doing; it is the gift of God"*).

3. Justifies and adopts believers into His family (Galatians 4:4-5, *"God sent His Son… so that we might receive adoption as sons"*).

Salvation Is Rooted in Christ's Work. Everything that God gives—forgiveness, righteousness, eternal life—comes only because of what Christ did on the cross. His death and resurrection made it possible for sinners to be reconciled to God and to be born again into His family.

This means that salvation is not about what we do—it is about what God has already done through Christ. Our role is simply to receive and believe what He has promised. Thus, to become a child of God is to be born of God—a transformation that He alone brings about by His power and grace.

Does Regeneration Come Before Faith or After?

There is a long-standing theological debate on whether regeneration (being born of God) happens before a person places their faith in Christ, or if faith is the catalyst that brings about regeneration.

1. **Regeneration Before Faith** – This view holds that a person must first be born of God before they can believe in Jesus. In other words, God sovereignly gives new life, enabling faith to follow.
2. **Faith Before Regeneration** – This view suggests that a person must first place their faith in Jesus, and then, as a result, God grants them new life (regeneration).

As the author of this book I obviously will express my view on this topic, and give my reasons for that choice. I believe the first view aligns best with Scripture. However, it's like dominoes falling— the first act (God regenerating the heart) sets everything else in motion, including faith.

Here's why:

1. *The Bible Describes Us as Spiritually Dead Before Salvation*

Ephesians 2:1 says: *"You were dead in the trespasses and sins in which you once walked."*

A spiritually dead person cannot initiate faith in Christ. Dead people do not respond to God unless He first brings them to life.

Jesus emphasised this in John 6:44: *"No one can come to me unless the Father who sent me draws him."*

If faith were something that a spiritually dead person could muster on their own, there would be no need for God to first act in their heart. *"unless the Father who sent me draws him."*

2. *Faith Itself is a Gift from God*

Ephesians 2:8-9 makes this clear: *"For by grace you have been saved through faith, and this is not your own doing; it is the gift of God, not a result of works, so that no one may boast."*

If faith is a gift from God, then it must be given to a person before they can believe—which suggests that regeneration (the giving of new life) comes before faith.

3. Regeneration is Described as a Sovereign Act of God

John 1:12-13 tells us that those who become children of God are "born, not of blood, nor of the will of the flesh, nor of the will of man, *but of God.*"

This birth is not something initiated by human effort, including faith—it is a work of God alone.

Similarly, in John 3:5-8, Jesus describes the new birth as something that comes by the Spirit's work, not by human will. He compares it to the wind, which blows where it pleases. We do not control it—it is God's sovereign work.

Therefore my conclusion is, Regeneration Precedes Faith.

Since faith is a response to God's grace, and since dead people cannot believe, it follows that God must first regenerate a person's heart before they are capable of believing in Jesus.

It's like dominoes falling—the first domino (regeneration) is pushed by God, and as a result, the next domino (faith) follows.

This view upholds the reality that salvation is entirely God's work. Our role is simply to respond to what He has already initiated.

Think of it this way:

Imagine you're out on the ocean in a yacht, enjoying the open sea. Suddenly, you notice a helicopter approaching. As it gets closer, you see a basket dangling from its undercarriage, and then you hear a voice over the P.A. system:

"You need to get into the basket immediately! A massive earthquake has triggered a tsunami—a 100-meter-high wave is coming toward you at 80 kilometres per hour. If you stay on your yacht, you will not survive. But if you get into the basket, we will take you back to the aircraft carrier, which can withstand the wave."

What Would You Do?

Without hesitation, as soon as the basket touches the yacht's deck, you would get in. Why? Because:

You received information—the helicopter crew told you about the danger.

You believed the warning—you understood the reality of the tsunami.

You trusted the rescue plan—you stepped into the basket.

Knowledge Leads to Action

Your action was based on knowing something to be true. You understood the consequences of staying on the yacht, and that understanding moved you to act. If the helicopter had never informed you of the coming disaster, you couldn't have acted at all.

Spiritual Parallel

This is exactly how faith in Christ works.

- It was God who took the first step by bringing you the Gospel message that warns us of our desperate condition and points us to the only rescue—Jesus Christ.
- Faith is believing and trusting in what God has revealed through His Word.
- Regeneration is like the helicopter arriving— God initiates the rescue by opening our hearts to the truth.
- Salvation is stepping into the basket—a response to God's gracious call.

Just as the knowledge of the tsunami led you to act, so God's work in our hearts leads us to embrace Christ by faith. Without that revelation, we would not act at all. We enacted, what we call our free will only after God revealed the truth to us by the Holy Spirit. Paul captures this reality in his message to the Corinthians:

"Where is the one who is wise? Where is the scribe? Where is the debater of this age? Has not God made foolish the wisdom of the world? For since, in the wisdom of God, the world did not know God through wisdom, it pleased God through the folly of what we preach to save those who believe. For Jews demand signs and Greeks seek wisdom, but we preach Christ crucified, a stumbling block to Jews and folly to Gentiles, **but to those who are called***, both Jews and Greeks, Christ the power of God and the wisdom of God. For the foolishness of God is wiser than men, and the weakness of God is stronger than men."* (1 Corinthians 1:20-25)

Three Responses to the Gospel.

Paul preached the message of the cross, and among those who heard it, there were two primary groups of people: Jews and Greeks (Gentiles). But within those two groups, there were three distinct responses to the Gospel:

1. The Jews sought signs – They demanded miracles as proof that the message was truly from God. They wanted supernatural evidence that aligned with their expectations of a powerful, conquering Messiah.

2. The Greeks saw it as foolishness – To them, the idea of a crucified Saviour was intellectual nonsense. It didn't fit with human wisdom or philosophy. They sought logical reasoning and worldly wisdom, and the cross seemed absurd.

3. The "called" responded in faith. They came from both Jewish and Greek backgrounds, yet something set them apart—they believed. To them, the message of the cross was not foolishness or weakness, but rather:

The power of God – A message that brings transformation, salvation, and new life.

The wisdom of God – A truth deeper than human understanding, revealing God's perfect plan.

So, what was the difference? The Call of God!

It wasn't the persuasive words of the the preacher, nor intellectual ability, or religious background that made the difference—it was God's calling that enabled them to believe.

This aligns with what Jesus said in John 6:44: *"No one can come to me unless the Father who sent me draws him."*

The calling of God is what changes a person's response to the Gospel. To some, the message remains foolishness or a stumbling block, but to those whom God calls, it becomes the very power and wisdom of God—bringing them into His family.

To understand who is "called" and how they are called, we need to look at the process God follows in salvation, which began in eternity past. Romans 8:28-30 outlines this process:

"And we know that for those who love God all things work together for good, for those who are called according to his purpose. For those whom he foreknew he also predestined to be conformed to the image of his Son, in order that he might be the firstborn among many brothers. And those whom he predestined he also called, and those whom he called he also justified, and those whom he justified he also glorified."

God's Stepping Stones in Salvation from God's view point.

This passage reveals a golden chain of salvation, an unbroken sequence that begins with God's eternal plan and ends in eternal glory:

1. Foreknowledge – God knew His people before they even existed. This does not simply mean He *knew in advance* who would choose Him,

but rather that He *set His love upon them* (Jeremiah 1:5, Ephesians 1:4-5) before they were born

2. Predestination – Those whom God foreknew, He predestined to be conformed to the image of Christ. This means He sovereignly determined that they would be transformed into Christlikeness. If we say this is because He "foreknew" who would believe and therefore He predestined those to be saved, it would completely changes the meaning of predestination.

Then it would only require Foreknow, Called, Justified, and Glorified. The word Predestination means to pre-(before the event) determine.

Romans 9:11 addresses this thought. *"though they were not yet born and had done nothing either good or bad—in order that God's purpose of election might continue, not because of works but because of him who calls"* God called Jacob rather than Esau.

3. Calling – Those whom He predestined, He also called. This is not just a general invitation, but an effective call—a summons that results in belief and salvation. This is the "call" Paul speaks of in 1 Corinthians 1:24, when the Gospel, though foolishness to many, is recognised by the called as *"the power and wisdom of God."*

4. Justification – Those whom He called, He also justified—declaring them righteous through faith in Christ. *"By sending his own Son in the likeness of sinful flesh and for sin, he condemned sin in the flesh, in order that the righteous requirement of the law might be fulfilled in us,"* Romans 8:3

5. Glorification – Those whom He justified, He also glorified. Though glorification will be finalised in the future, Paul speaks of it in the past tense because our glorification has started, *"....beholding the glory of the Lord, are being transformed into the same image from one degree of glory to another. For this comes from the Lord who is the Spirit."* 2 Corinthians 3:18

God's Sovereign Choice:

This passage presents a difficult truth for many because it challenges the idea that humans are in full control of their salvation. We often see ourselves as self-determining creatures, believing that we make the ultimate choice in matters of faith. But this passage clearly states that:

1. Some will respond to the call, believe, and be justified—not because of any human qualification but purely as an act of God's grace.

2. It is God who initiates salvation, choosing people before they ever choose Him.

This may be challenging to reconcile with human reasoning, but we must remember that the Bible does not present truths for us to ignore simply because they are difficult. The Holy Spirit inspired the Apostle Paul to write this for a reason—not for us to debate endlessly, but to cause us to humbly worship the God who saves.

Though we may struggle with the mystery of God's sovereign choice, one thing remains clear: salvation is an act of God's grace from beginning to end. And for those who are called, it is a reality that brings deep assurance—because what God begins, He will complete (Philippians 1:6).

So, what is it that makes some people understand the gospel and embrace it, when others have no desire to do the same? What awakens and enlightens people? It's the Holy Spirit. Jesus sent the Holy Spirit for this purpose, as he told His disciples. *"And when he comes, he will convict the world concerning sin and righteousness and judgment: concerning sin, because they do not believe in me;* John 16:8-9.

Referring to the illustration of the yacht, we could have stayed on the yacht but knowing what we were facing sealed our choice. It was awareness that made all the difference. Someone external to us took the initiative to let us know. Without that act we would never have been aware. But once we realised, we acted.

With the Christian gospel, it is not human reason or gifted speakers that make it easy to understand. It happens through the work of the Holy Spirit in our lives. It is God that will break into indifferent, resistant, or ignorant hearts and let His light shine revealing the glory and the beauty of Jesus. When that occurs hearts will embrace the saviour of this world, the Lord Jesus Christ. It is God that birthed them into His family.

"he gave the right to become children of God, who were born,...of God" verse 12,13.

The Call to Share the Gospel with Everyone.

While the Bible teaches that God sovereignly calls people to salvation, it is crucial to remember that we do not know who the "called" are. Because of this, our responsibility is not to determine who will respond but to faithfully proclaim the Gospel to all people.

Jesus gave us the Great Commission in Matthew 28:19-20:

"Go therefore and make disciples of all nations, baptising them in the name of the Father and of the Son and of the Holy Spirit, teaching them to observe all that I have commanded you."

This command is for all believers—we are to present the Gospel to everyone, trusting that God will work in the hearts of those He is calling.

Take the example of Paul. On the day Paul travelled to Damascus to bring Christians back to Jerusalem for trial, he certainly did not begin the day thinking, todays is the day I will become a Christian. Yet, God revealed Himself to Paul, and he believed—all as an act of His grace. Paul, who strongly believed in God's sovereignty in salvation, was one of the most passionate evangelists. He tirelessly preached to all people, knowing that God's call would be effective in the lives of those He had chosen. He wrote: *"I endure everything for the sake of the elect, that they also may obtain the salvation that is in Christ Jesus with eternal glory."* (2 Timothy 2:10)

Even though Paul understood that God had already chosen His people, he also knew that their salvation would come through the preaching of the Gospel.

Faith Comes by Hearing.

Paul also wrote in Romans 10:14-15, 17:

"How then will they call on Him in whom they have not believed? And how are they to believe in Him of whom they have never heard? And how are they to hear without someone preaching? And how are they to preach unless they are sent? As it is written, 'How beautiful are the feet of those who preach the good news!' ... So faith comes from hearing, and hearing through the word of Christ."

Our Responsibility: Proclaim, Not Predict

We do not know who will respond, but God does.

We are called to share the Gospel with everyone and trust that God will do the work in people's hearts.

Some will reject the message, but others will hear and believe—because God is calling them.

God's sovereignty in salvation does not eliminate our responsibility to evangelise. Instead, it motivates us—because we know that our labour is not in vain. As we faithfully share the Gospel, God is at work, calling people to Himself.

We sow the seed, but it is God who makes it grow (1 Corinthians 3:6-7).

Again I say, Our Responsibility is to Proclaim, Not to Predict!

5. Follow

5. The fifth action that embracing Jesus brings is

WE FOLLOW HIM:

"One of the two who heard John speak and *followed* Jesus was Andrew, Simon Peter's brother." 1:40. "The next day Jesus decided to go to Galilee. He found Philip and said to him, "*Follow me.*"" 1:43.

Jesus was seeking followers and chapter one ends with 5 followers. John, Andrew, Peter, Philip, and Nathanael. In the next 11 chapters we will see that invitation to follow Jesus extended to many. There are varied responses. Some walk away, others take inquiring steps, still others embrace Jesus knowing full well that it may cost them their lives.

Following Jesus is not the same as supporting a football or a basketball or any other sporting team, where people come to sit on the sideline and cheer for their team. The word explains itself. In following, you copy the actions of the person you are following. *"Be imitators of me, as I am of Christ."* was how Paul put it. (1 Corinthians 11:1.)

When it came to commitment, Jesus didn't mince His words as can be seen in Luke 14:26 *"If anyone comes to me and does not hate his own father and mother and wife and children and brothers and sisters, yes, and even his own life, he cannot be my disciple. Whoever does not bear his own cross and come after me cannot be my disciple."*

These words will jar the minds of any reader. However, they need to be seen in the idiom of His day. It's comparative love. It calls us to favour one above the other. Following Jesus meant that He needs to be seen as our first love and all other loves or relationship take second place. When things compete for our time, Jesus gets first right of claim. That is before our father, or mother, or wife, or husband, or any other relative. Again, we turn back to the parable that Jesus told us to illustrate this. Remember the man finding a treasure in a field and then going and selling everything he had just to get the treasure that was in the field. Selling everything because there is something far more valuable. That treasure is Jesus, and we prize Him so highly that we will do anything to have Him, because He is the most prized treasure of our lives. Matthew 13:44 *"The kingdom of heaven is like treasure hidden in a field. When a man found it, he hid it again, and then in his joy went and sold all he had and bought that field."*

Being a Follower is simple putting Jesus at the forefront of every decision, priority, and relationship. When it comes to priorities, Jesus laid them out in Matthew 28. Here we will find the demands that Christ places on all who follow Him. *"And Jesus came and said to them, "All authority in heaven and on earth has been given to me. Go therefore and make disciples of all nations, baptising them in the name of the Father and of the Son and of the Holy Spirit, teaching them to observe all that I have commanded you. And behold, I am with you always, to the end of the age."* A Follower takes the message of Jesus and talks about it within his or her work-a-day world.

So, a follower is a disciple, which means a learner. We are to learn from the teachings of Jesus, so we know how we are to live in this world where He has left us. We know that this world is hostile to Christ followers but remember the prayer of Jesus to His and our Father in John 17:15-*18 "I do not ask that you take them out of the world, but that you keep them from the evil one. They are not of the world, just as I am not of the world. Sanctify them in the truth; your word is truth. As you sent me into the world, so I have sent them into the world. And for their sake I consecrate myself, that they also may be sanctified in truth."*

Jesus' prayers are always answered by the Father. But we will never experience that prayer being answered in our life unless we place ourselves in a situation where we need it.

Identity

Followers declare their relationship with Jesus by baptism. After believing and receiving Christ, as the Bible shows, followers were baptised.

Acts 2:41 *"So those who received his word were baptised, and there were added that day about three thousand souls."*

Acts 8:12 *"But when they believed Philip as he preached the good news about the kingdom of God and the name of Jesus Christ, they were baptised, both men and women."*

Acts 18:8 *"Crispus, the ruler of the synagogue, believed in the Lord, together with his entire household. And many of the Corinthians hearing Paul believed and were baptised."*

There is a pattern here, *"They believed and were baptised"* that's why we call it Believers Baptism. So why baptism? Good question. What do you do with dead people? You bury them. A believer's baptism demonstrates what has happened to them spiritually in a mental and visual way. We have died, which is the wages or consequences of sin (Romans 6:23) but our death occurred over 2,000 years ago, *"Now if we have died with Christ, we believe that we will also live with him."*. Romans 6:8 *"We were buried therefore with him by baptism into death, in order that, just as Christ was raised from the dead by the glory of the Father, we too might walk in newness of life"*. Romans 6:4.

Baptism illustrates the two great truths of being in Christ. The first is that we have died in Christ as far as God is concerned. Therefore, the debt of sin has been paid. This is illustrated when a believer is placed under the waters of baptism. It is the picture that the dead person has been buried. Secondly by coming up out of the water, we illustrate the believer's resurrection to a new life, a life that is lived for Christ because He is our life. Baptism does nothing more than illustrate this spiritual truth. This is not how we are placed into Christ's death, that is the work of the Holy Spirit, a reality that took place when Jesus died on the cross over two thousand years ago. Remember, God in His foreknowledge knew who would be redeemed. Followers don't just learn they teach. *"Teach what I have taught you"*, were Jesus' words, and we are responsible for doing that as well. Paul put it to Timothy this way: *"You then, my son, be strong in the grace that is in Christ Jesus. And the things you have heard me say in the presence of many witnesses entrust to reliable people who will also be qualified to teach others."* Paul reiterates it in verses 24-26 and sets some perimeters to govern our approach. *"And the Lord's servant must not be quarrelsome but must be kind to everyone, able to teach, not resentful. Opponents must be gently instructed, in the hope that God will grant them repentance leading them to a knowledge of the truth, and that they will come to their senses and escape from the trap of the devil, who has taken them captive to do his will."* Being a Follower is being a learner and no one really learns without teaching.

Identity

Here are 10 discussion questions based on our notes: Chapter 2

Identity in Christ:

1. What does John 1:12 mean when it says we "become" children of God?

    - How does the illustration of metamorphosis (grub to butterfly) help explain spiritual transformation?

2. John 1:13 outlines three ways we do *not* become children of God. What are they, and why are these misconceptions common in religious culture?

3. Why is it vital to understand that spiritual birth is not inherited, achieved, or bestowed through rituals?

    - What are the risks of misunderstanding this?

4. Reflecting on Ephesians 2:1 and John 6:44, why is regeneration (spiritual rebirth) necessary before someone can place faith in Christ?

5. Using the tsunami and helicopter analogy, explain the relationship between revelation, faith, and action in salvation.

    - How does this illustrate the work of the Holy Spirit?

6. What role does the Holy Spirit play in a person's ability to understand, believe, and respond to the Gospel?

    - Why is human reasoning insufficient without Him?

7. Romans 8:28–30 presents a "golden chain" of salvation. List the five stages and explain how they build a picture of God's sovereign work from eternity to eternity.

8. What does it mean to truly *follow* Jesus, based on John 1:43 and Luke 14:26?

    o How does this differ from merely being a fan or admirer?

9. Why is baptism described as a picture, not a means, of salvation?

    o How does believer's baptism visually communicate spiritual realities?

10. In what ways are disciples also teachers?

- Reflect on Paul's instructions to Timothy. How are you personally engaging in passing on what you've learned to others?

Identity

Al Watson

Chapter Three: Jesus the Word

John describes Jesus by using 12 words or titles to introduce Jesus to us.

In our study we are going to look at each of the names or titles, so as we get to know Jesus better. The obvious question that we ask is, how well do you have to know Jesus to be born again? If you take the thief on the cross as an example, one will assume that this was the first time he had encountered Jesus. It's true that he might have heard about him, but it's unlikely that the thief moved in the same circles as Jesus.

Yet he at one stage during the crucifixion turned to Jesus and said, *"remember me when you come into your kingdom"* Jesus replied, *"This day you will be with me in paradise."* There was some point in the events of the cross where this man recognised who Jesus was. Remember that is where you start the process or journey in believing in Jesus and being born again as a child of God and becoming a follower of Jesus.

Let me also say that this recognition only occurs when the Holy Spirit enables people to see who Jesus is. As we go through the 12 chapters of John, you will see that there were people seeing and hearing the same things, but some believed, and some didn't. Same evidence, same message yet two very different responses to Jesus.

Recognising who Jesus is goes beyond mere intellectual understanding. Again and again, we see that the Holy Spirit works in a person's mind, enabling them to recognise Jesus and believe in Him.

We also discover that it is through the Word of God that we come to recognise Jesus. Unlike in the past, when He physically walked the earth in Israel, we cannot go to Him in person. The only way to know who Jesus claimed to be is through the testimony of the men and women who lived and interacted with Him 2,000 years ago—a testimony recorded in the New Testament. The Bible is the primary resource the Holy Spirit uses to reveal Jesus Christ, the Son of God, to us.

As Paul wrote, *"Faith comes by hearing, and hearing through the Word of Christ"* (Romans 10:17). Similarly, in the parable of the sower (Luke 8:11), Jesus explained that *"the seed is the Word of God."* Just as a farmer scatters seed in a field, the Gospel message is sown in people's hearts as they hear it.

As we see from John 20:31 John wrote this Gospel so that people would believe. And it's my belief that the more you know about the person of Jesus Christ the Son of God, the stronger your faith in Him will be. The better you know Him the more you will trust Him and embrace Him and be willing to follow Him.

So, let's get start with the first of the 12 names or titles that John uses to introduce us to Jesus. he First is the Word: *"In the beginning was the Word."*

Why does John use the title "Word" to describe Jesus?

Is he drawing us back to the opening words of Genesis—*"In the beginning, God created the heavens and the earth"*? Is John suggesting that Jesus has come to bring about a new beginning? I believe that is precisely his point. Just as there was a beginning at creation, now there is a new beginning through Jesus.

The Greek word for "Word" is *Logos*. Greek philosophers often spoke of the *logos* as the rational order, the natural law, the underlying logic of reality. In Greek thought, the universe functioned according to this impersonal principle. To them, *logos* was the wisdom behind the cosmos.

John takes this familiar concept and redefines it. He does something similar to what Paul did at Mars Hill when he discovered a shrine inscribed with *"To the unknown god."* Paul used that cultural reference as a bridge, explaining to his audience that this *unknown god* was, in fact, Jesus. He adapted a common idea to help his listeners grasp the truth.

John does the same here. If the culture of the time understood *logos* as a mysterious force behind the universe, he would use that very concept to reveal the true identity of Jesus.

But John goes even further. He declares that this mysterious wisdom—the *logos*—not only pre-existed creation and governed the universe but was *with* God and, in fact, *was* God. Then, in a revelation that would astonish both Hebrew and Greek thinkers, he proclaims that this Word became flesh.

The *logos* is not an abstract, formless force. Nor is it an impersonal principle. The Word is a living, knowable, eternal being—one who desires a relationship with His people.

There is also the idea that words communicate thoughts…

Words Communicate.

People understand what I am thinking through the words I use to express my ideas. In the same way, Jesus, as the Word, reveals to us the mind of God. As John writes in verse 18: *"No one has ever seen God; the only God, who is at the Father's side—He has made Him known."* (John 1:18)

Philip, one of the twelve disciples, once said to Jesus, *"Lord, show us the Father, and that will be enough for us."* Jesus responded:

"Have I been with you so long, and still you do not know me, Philip? Whoever has seen me has seen the Father. How can you say, 'Show us the Father'?" (John 14:8-9)

The Word is God, yet He is also the part of God that took on flesh so that we could truly know Him. The best way to understand "the God who is" is by seeing Him through the life and teachings of Jesus Christ.

Just as you know what I am thinking by what I say, we know God through His Word—Jesus.

"In the beginning was the Word, and the Word was with God, and the Word was God."

This statement also reveals that God is not a singular personality. The Word was with God, yet the Word was God. The terms "with" and "was" tell us a great deal about who God is. Later in John's Gospel, we are introduced to the third person of the Godhead—the Holy Spirit.

Thus, we see the mystery of the Trinity: one God in three persons—Father, Son, and Holy Spirit.

The Word Became Flesh

For me, the greatest miracle of all is this: the Word became flesh. John 1:14 declares: *"And the Word became flesh and dwelt among us, and we have seen His glory, glory as of the only Son from the Father, full of grace and truth."*

Jesus Became Fully Human

Hebrews 2:14 *"Since therefore the children share in flesh and blood, He Himself likewise partook of the same things."*

Hebrews 2:17 *"Therefore, He had to be made like His brothers in every respect..."*

This means that although Jesus is God, He had to become human to bear the judgment of a holy God for the sins of a fallen humanity. He had to be fully human because it was humans that had disobeyed God and were facing judgment. Also, only a human could experience death. Which is why the Scripture says, *"He had to be made like His brothers in every respect."*

The Humility of Christ

Al Watson

Philippians 2:6-8

"Who, though He was in the form of God, did not count equality with God a thing to be grasped, but emptied Himself, by taking the form of a servant, being born in the likeness of men. And being found in human form, He humbled Himself by becoming obedient to the point of death, even death on a cross."

Notice the phrase: "being born in human form."

How are children born in human form? Through the very process that God the Son Himself went through to become the man Christ Jesus.

This raises an important question: What does it mean to be human? What are we made of, and how are we made?

We know that our bodies are made up of cells—around 100 trillion of them. Each cell contains 46 chromosomes, which are long strands of letter sequences. These sequences consist of only four letters (A, C, G, & T), yet they are arranged in such a way that they form the blueprint of our bodies—our DNA.

DNA determines our height, eye colour, skin colour, and the structure of our skeleton and nervous system. It ensures that every nerve is correctly connected to the brain. It orchestrates the plumbing of our circulatory system, guiding the formation of arteries and veins that transport blood throughout the body, and a thousand other needs.

This incredibly intricate design system ensures that:

- The energy from the food we eat is distributed to the right muscles through our bloodstream.
- The oxygen filtered by our lungs is mixed with blood and carried throughout the body.
- Waste products are efficiently removed via the organs designed for that purpose.

Identity

The most remarkable part? We don't have to think about any of this—DNA controls it all.

Truly, the Bible speaks accurately when it declares:

"For You created my inmost being You knit me together in my mother's womb. I praise You because I am fearfully and wonderfully made." (Psalm 139:13-14)

The Living Bible paraphrases this scripture this way.

"You made all the delicate, inner parts of my body, and knit them all together in my mother's womb. Thank you for making me so wonderfully complex! It's amazing to think about. Your workmanship is marvellous— and how well I know it."

Each cell in our body contains around 3 billion letters of DNA. As we have said these letters form long strands, and if we were to stretch out the DNA from just one cell into a single line, it would measure nearly 6 feet (182 cm) in length.

Now, consider this: if you took all the DNA sequences from the 30-40 trillion cells in your body and laid them end to end in a single continuous thread, it would reach the sun and back over 600 times. That's a journey of 93 million miles (150 million km) multiplied by 600!

We are truly fearfully and wonderfully made!

And it all begins with just one living cell—containing 46 chromosomes.

- 23 chromosomes come from your mother, contributed through the ovum.
- 23 chromosomes come from your father, contributed through the sperm.

You are a unique blend of both your parents. As soon as conception occurs, this single cell begins to divide and multiply, forming new cells that continue this blending process. Over the next nine months, these cells keep dividing and developing, ultimately forming a fully developed baby—ready to leave the womb and enter the world.

And once born, this child will continue to grow until reaching the full capacity set by their DNA. That's how you and I came into this world.

But how was Jesus the Word conceived?

This is a great mystery, but it is a mystery that can be explored—both through Scripture and science. The first thing the Bible tells us is that Jesus was born of a virgin. Luke 1:34 *"And Mary said to the angel, 'How will this be, since I am a virgin?"*

The angel answered her question: Luke 1:35 *"The Holy Spirit will come upon you, and the power of the Most High will overshadow you; therefore, the child to be born will be called holy—the Son of God."*

So, Mary was pregnant—yet she was still a virgin. Joseph was not the father, nor was any other man. In Mary's womb, an ovum was fertilised, but not in the way that occurs in normal conception. In this miraculous event, it was God the Son—the Word—who became the male contribution in Mary's conception. He didn't contribute the seed; He became the seed that fertilised Mary's ovum.

So, this does not mean that a fourth divine being was created (Father, Son, Holy Spirit, and Jesus). Rather, it means that God the Son took on humanity within Himself. And—thankfully—He never removed it, even after His death, burial, and resurrection.

Now, in heaven, we have a Godman who truly understands what it means to be human. This is why the book of Hebrews says:

"For we do not have a high priest who is unable to sympathise with our weaknesses, but one who in every respect has been tempted as we are, yet without sin. Let us then with confidence draw near to the throne of grace, that we may receive mercy and find grace to help in time of need." Hebrews 4:15-16

Identity

Jesus understands what it means to be human.

God the Son allowed Himself to become part of the very human reproductive process that He had created in the first place—so that He could dwell among us. For nine months, that one miraculous cell—containing both human DNA and divine DNA—divided and multiplied, growing until the baby Jesus was ready to be born in Bethlehem. Fully God and fully man.

As John declares: John 1:14 *"And the Word became flesh and dwelt among us, and we beheld His glory, glory as of the only begotten Son of God."*

This is precisely what is meant in John 3:16: *"For God so loved the world that <u>He gave</u> His only Son…"*

Or in the words of Isaiah the prophet:

Isaiah 9:6 *"For to us a child is born,"* (let me add a word to show the contrast BUT) *"to us a Son is given."* The Son pre-existed, for to be given He had to exist, it was the child that was the new creation.

And again, in Isaiah 7:14: *"Therefore, the Lord Himself will give you a sign. Behold, the virgin shall conceive and bear a Son and shall call His name Immanuel."* (*Immanuel* means *God with us*.)

There has never been a human being like Jesus Christ. He is the sinless Son of God, born of the virgin Mary over 2,000 years ago, to become the Saviour of the world.

Some might ask: *If all humans have a sinful nature, and Mary was a human being, and Jesus was born of Mary—how could He be sinless?*

That's a good question.

The Roman Catholic Religion answers it by teaching that Mary herself was conceived without sin— through what they call the Immaculate Conception—so that she could bear a sinless child.

But this explanation doesn't solve the issue. If Mary had to be immaculately conceived to be sinless, then wouldn't her mother also have needed an immaculate conception? And her grandmother? And so on, all the way back to Eve before the fall? I believe the Bible and biology give us an answer.

We ask the question: Where does life come from? How is it created?

The Bible answers this by saying that life is in the blood. This does not mean that blood itself is life, but rather that the mysterious essence of life resides in the blood. This goes beyond simply saying that we need blood to stay alive—it suggests that the very germ of life is what generates the blood in our circulatory system.

We turn to the book of Leviticus, which provides crucial insight into this concept. The context of Leviticus revolves around the sacrificial system—God's provision to deal with the guilt and debt of sin that humanity accumulates.

Although Leviticus speaks of animals and their blood, the principle applies to humans as well:

Leviticus 17:11 *"For the life of the flesh is in the blood, and I have given it for you on the altar to make atonement for your souls, for it is the blood that makes atonement by the life."*

Leviticus 17:14 *"For the life of every creature is its blood: its blood is its life."*

Consider the connection between blood, sin, and atonement and what it means? We know from Scripture that sin carries a penalty—death:

Romans 6:23 *"For the wages of sin is death..."*

If death is the penalty for sin, then the only way that debt can be paid is through death. However, God provided a temporary way for people in the Old Testament to deal with their guilt—through animal sacrifices.

These sacrifices foreshadowed the coming of Jesus Christ, the true Lamb of God:

John 1:29 *"Behold, the Lamb of God, who takes away the sin of the world!"*

Yet, the blood of animals could never remove sin:

Hebrews 10:4 *"For it is impossible for the blood of bulls and goats to take away sins."*

So why did God command sacrifices?

The sacrificial system was designed to teach two key truths:

1. The animal's death represents what should happen to the person offering the sacrifice.
2. The animal acts as a temporary substitute for the sinner—pointing forward to Christ, who would ultimately die for the sins of the world.

When the animal died in place of the person, the person was no longer alienated from God but could be "at one" with Him. That is the meaning of the word atonement; at-one-ment.

If life is in the blood, as Scripture states, then how is blood itself created? There was a medical doctor who wrote a book many years ago, called *"The Chemistry of the Blood."* He was Dr M.R. DeHaan. Let me

quote Dr De Haan.

"It is now definitely known that the blood which flows in an unborn babies arteries and veins is not derived from the mother but is produced within the body of the foetus itself only after the introduction of the male sperm. An unfertilised ovum can never develop blood since the female egg does not by itself contain the elements essential for the production of this blood. It is only after the male element has entered the ovum that blood can develop."

Then Dr DeHaan uses a simple illustration of a 4-day old hen egg that is being incubated. Dr DeHaan again;

"As a very simple illustration of this, think of the egg of a hen. An unfertilised egg is just an ovum on a much larger scale than the human ovum. You may incubate this unfertilised hen's egg, but it will never develop. It will decay and become rotten, but no chick will result. Let that egg be fertilised by the introduction of the male sperm and incubation will bring to light the presence of LIFE IN THAT EGG.

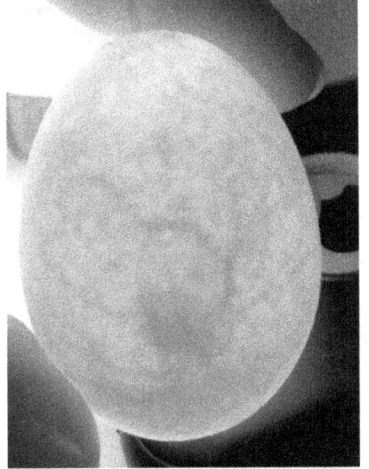

After a few hours it visibly develops.

In a little while red streaks occur in the egg denoting the presence of Blood. This can never occur and does never occur until THE MALE SPERM HAS BEEN UNITED WITH THE FEMALE The male element has added life to the egg. Life is in the blood according to scripture, for Moses says: "For the life of the flesh is in the blood. .*

Leviticus 17:11.

"Since there is no life in the egg until the male sperm unites with it, and the life is in the blood, it follows that the male sperm is the source of the blood, the seed of life."

What does that mean when looking at the birth of Jesus, and the Transmission of Sin and the Uniqueness of Christ's Birth?

When a child is in the womb, not one ounce of blood from the mother is in the veins of the child. The DNA for making blood comes from the male. Therefore, the life factor is passed to each generation by males.

Adam passed on his sinful nature to all his descendants, both male and female, as Scripture indicates: "Therefore, just as sin came into the world through one man, and death through sin, and so death spread to all men because all sinned—" (Romans 5:12).

Because the life factor is transmitted through the man, and that life is in the blood, it follows that fathers pass life from one generation to the next. This is how the sin nature is passed down through humanity. However, in the case of Jesus, no human male was involved in His conception. The male contribution in Mary's womb was not from a sinful man, but from the sinless Son of God Himself. **He was the seed.**

His flesh—His full humanity—came from Mary. His divine nature and His perfect, sinless life came because He is the God the Son.

Mary's qualification to be the mother of Jesus was that she belonged to the family line of King David, fulfilling prophecy. While she was undoubtedly a godly young woman, she was not sinless. Thus, the life of Jesus was the Son of God incarnate—fully God and fully man.

This is why we speak of *"the precious blood of Christ"* (1 Peter 1:19). His blood was not tainted by sin—it was the blood/life of the sinless Son of God. Theologians refer to this profound mystery as the hypostatic union—the reality that Jesus is both fully God and fully man.

Al Watson

Here are 10 questions based on our notes: Chapter 2

1. Recognising Jesus – The thief on the cross recognised Jesus in his final moments. How does this demonstrate the role of the Holy Spirit in bringing people to faith? What does this teach us about salvation?

2. Faith Through the Word – John 20:31 states that John wrote his Gospel so people might believe. How does the Bible serve as the primary way for people to recognise Jesus today?

3. Jesus as "The Word" – Why does John introduce Jesus as "The Word" (Logos)? How does this connect to both Greek philosophy and the Jewish understanding of God's revelation?

4. Jesus as Fully God and Fully Man – Why was it necessary for Jesus to be both fully divine and fully human? How does this affect our understanding of salvation?

5. The Incarnation – John 1:14 declares, "The Word became flesh and dwelt among us." What does this reveal about God's desire for a relationship with humanity?

6. Faith and Evidence – Many people in Jesus' time saw His miracles, yet some believed while others rejected Him. Why do you think people respond differently to the same evidence?

7. The Transmission of Sin – Romans 5:12 states that sin entered the world through Adam. How does the virgin birth of Jesus ensure that He remained sinless?

8. Believing vs. Receiving – John 1:12-13 speaks of both believing in Jesus and receiving Him. What is the difference between these two, and why are both necessary for salvation?

9. The Role of the Holy Spirit —The notes emphasise that the Holy Spirit enables people to recognise Jesus. How does the Spirit work in our hearts and minds to bring about faith?

10. Living as a Child of God —Once we believe and receive Jesus, we become children of God. How should this identity shape our daily lives and interactions with others?

Al Watson

Chapter Four: Jesus is God

The Word Became Flesh and Dwelt Among Us

Look again at John 1:14:

"And the Word became flesh and dwelt among us."

The word translated "dwelt" literally means "to live in a tent" or "to tabernacle among us."

In the Old Testament, the Tabernacle was the place where people could meet with God. Now, John reveals that through Jesus—the Word—people can truly meet with God. This is the very reason why the Word became flesh—why Jesus took on humanity.

What was lost in the fall of man in the Garden of Eden could now be restored. As 2 Corinthians 5:19 declares: *"God was in Christ reconciling the world to Himself."*

Recognising and Receiving Jesus.

This is the Jesus that John calls us to believe in. Believing is recognising who He is, and acknowledging with thankfulness what He has done for us via the cross. Trusting that death to have paid our pending condemnation.

Believing in Jesus is to receive Him. It is to embrace Him as God, to trust Him as our Saviour, and to depend on Him to restore our broken relationship with God.

When we believe and receive Jesus, we become children of God—part of God's eternal family. As God's children, we now seek to follow Jesus, learning from Him. We learn of Jesus by studying the Bible. As we discover the truth within His teaching, we reflect that truth in the way we live, and we share it with others.

"The Word was with God, and the Word was God. He was with God in the beginning." John 1:1-2

John records that the Word was with God but was also God Himself, meaning there is no difference between God and the Word—both are God. We know we are talking about Jesus here because verse 14 shows that *"the Word became flesh and dwelt among us"*— *"we have seen his glory, glory as of the only Son from the Father, full of grace and truth."*

John, in this Gospel, sets out the theology of the deity of Jesus Christ. The God of the Bible is the Triune God—One God in three persons: Father, Son, and Holy Spirit.

The point of John's Gospel is that salvation can only come to us if we believe in and receive Jesus. And the Jesus we believe in and receive is God. We need to recognise Jesus for who He is—God in the Flesh. As Martin Luther used to say, "It's the Big God who became small."

To understand the deity of Christ, we must revisit the purpose behind John's Gospel. John 20:30-31

"Now Jesus did many other signs in the presence of the disciples, which are not written in this book; but these are written so that you may believe that Jesus is the Christ, the Son of God, and that by believing you may have life in his name."

That question is begging an answer from us: *"Do you believe that Jesus is the Christ, the Son of God?"*

It must have an answer if we are to become followers of Jesus.

Do you believe that Jesus is God? God the Son?

Also, we need to understand what is meant by *"having life in His Name"*.

Identity

When we speak about names in our world, they mean little more than a way to identify people. What is your name? This is how we distinguish one person from another.

But when you look at what is meant in the Bible, it is far more than a point of identification. Here, the word "name" means "the sum total of who I am." So, salvation comes to us because we believe in the sum total of all that Jesus is. We believe and embrace all that the Bible reveals to us about the person of Jesus Christ.

Tragically, the Jesus that is being preached by many people today is much less than the sum total of all that Jesus is.

Let's look at how the Bible uses the idea of believing in the name to represent the sum of the person being spoken of. It's not just a way to identify a person—it is speaking about everything that person is.

One of the best places to understand what is meant by "believing in His Name" is to go to Exodus 3. Moses is standing before the burning bush, asking God, "What is your name?" Remember, Moses has just been commissioned to go back to Egypt and bring the nation of Israel out of their slavery. Moses knows that he will be asked, "Who is this God that has told you to do this?" Expecting that kind of question, Moses asks God, "Who shall I say sent me? What is your Name?"

God answers Moses in two ways. 1st—He tells Moses that He can't be reduced to a name: "I Am who I AM." I am the sum total of all that I am. That's who I am.

Within this "I AM" title is the idea that God is the Eternal, Existent One.

God does not say "I WAS" or "I WILL BE", but He says "I AM"—it's in the present tense.

This is because there is no past or future with God—God is always present. He is the self-existent, sovereign Creator and Preserver of all that is—the Great I AM.

However, if "I AM" has more to do with God's identity as the Eternal Existent One, does God have a Name? Yes, He does. God uses many names to reveal Himself to us.

On this occasion with Moses, He gives us the name LORD, or "Yahweh". When you read the Bible and see LORD in capital letters, that's the word Yahweh—the Covenant name of God, which speaks of God's sovereign authority. He is the Boss. He is in control.

"My Name is THE LORD" (or Yahweh in Hebrew). Exodus 3:15.

"God also said to Moses, 'Say this to the people of Israel: The Lord, the God of your fathers, the God of Abraham, the God of Isaac, and the God of Jacob, has sent me to you.' This is my name forever, and thus I am to be remembered throughout all generations."

So, God's answer to Moses' question, "What is your Name?", was:

"I AM everything that my names mean."

When you come to the New Testament; the term "name" is used as shorthand for "all that God is" when referring to Jesus. For example: Acts 4:12 *"And there is salvation in no one else, for there is no other name under heaven given among men by which we must be saved."*

When Peter spoke to the first Non-Jewish person to become a Christ Follower- Cornelius, he said this, " *'Truly I understand that God shows no partiality, but in every nation, anyone who fears him and does what is right is acceptable to him. As for the word that he sent to Israel, preaching good news of peace through Jesus Christ (he is Lord of all), you yourselves know what happened throughout all Judea, beginning from Galilee after the baptism that John proclaimed: how God anointed Jesus of Nazareth with the Holy Spirit and with power. He went about doing good and healing all who were oppressed by the devil, for God was with him. And we are witnesses of all that he did both in the country of the Jews and in Jerusalem.*

They put him to death by hanging him on a tree, but God raised him on the third day and made him to appear, not to all the people but to us who had been chosen by God as witnesses, who ate and drank with him after he rose from the dead. And he commanded us to preach to the people and to testify that he is the one appointed by God to be judge of the living and the dead. To him, all the prophets bear witness that everyone who believes in him receives forgiveness of sins <u>through his name</u>.'" Acts 10:34-43.

Then you have Pauls letter to the believers at Corinth where he reminds them they *"were justified in the name of the Lord Jesus Christ and by the Spirit of our God."*

1 Corinthians 6:9-11 *"Or do you not know that the unrighteous will not inherit the kingdom of God? Do not be deceived: neither the sexually immoral, nor idolaters, nor adulterers, nor men who practice homosexuality, nor thieves, nor the greedy, nor drunkards, nor slanderers, nor robbers will inherit the kingdom of God. And such were some of you. But you were washed, you were sanctified, <u>you were justified in the name</u> of the Lord Jesus Christ and by the Spirit of our God."*

You were washed, sanctified, justified.

Becoming a Christian means that you believe that Jesus is God, equal with the Father and the Holy Spirit. And if you doubt that we need to believe that Jesus is God, have a look at what Jesus says in. John 8:21-24: *"So he said to them again, 'I am going away, and you will seek me, and you will die in your sin. Where I am going, you cannot come.' So, the Jews said, 'Will he kill himself, since he says, 'Where I am going, you cannot come'?' He said to them, 'You are from below; I am from above. You are of this world; I am not of this world. I told you that you would die in your sins, for unless you believe that I AM (some translations add "he" here, but it is not in the original Greek text), you will die in your sins.'"*

Jesus is claiming to be God, look at what the religious leaders did after Jesus claimed to be the "I AM" in verse 59: *"So they picked up stones to throw at him, but Jesus hid himself and went out of the temple."* As far as they were concerned, for a man to claim to be God was "blasphemy", which carried the death penalty—that's why they picked up stones, desiring to stone Jesus to death.

To reinforce Jesus' identity, John repeatedly connects God's declaration, "I AM that I AM," with Jesus— eight times—to show that they are one and the same. The God who spoke to Moses is the same God revealed as Jesus.

These "I AM" statements are not merely Jesus saying, "Hey, I'm talking about myself here." While they do identify Him, they also invoke the divine name revealed at the Burning Bush. The religious leaders certainly understood what Jesus meant by using the "I AM" title—so much so that they sought to stone Him for blasphemy.

It's important that we understand that it's not our faith that saves us— Jesus saves us, and He saves us because of who He is. You will notice that the first "I AM" is about bread. The idea is clear. When you eat bread, to take it inside of you where you reap the benefits as it energises your body; it sustains life.

The same is true with Jesus—you need to receive Him. You need to be united with Him. Through the Spirit, Jesus needs to be in you to be saved.

Jesus also uses the illustration of water in the same way when He says: *"Whoever believes in me shall never thirst."* It's water that you take into yourself that quenches your thirst.

Jesus put it this way in John 14:20 *"In that day you will know that I am in my Father, and you in me, and I in you."*

Repeatedly in the New Testament, we read the words "in Christ". Here are just a few examples for you to look up: Ephesians 2:10; 2:13; Colossians 2:6-7; 3:3.

Identity

The "I AM" Passages in John's Gospel:

Here are the eight "I AM" passages that Jesus uses to describe Himself. Notice how they build on the truth that Jesus is the God of the Burning Bush, where He revealed Himself as "I AM that I AM."

1. John 6:35 *"I AM the Bread of Life. Whoever comes to me shall not hunger, and whoever believes in me shall never thirst."*
2. John 8:12 *"I AM the Light of the World. Whoever follows me shall not walk in darkness but will have the light of life."*
3. John 8:58 *"Jesus said to them, 'Truly, truly, I say to you, before Abraham was, I AM.'"*

As we have said already, you only have to look at the reaction of the religious leaders to these statement to know that they knew Jesus was claiming to be God.

"Jesus said, 'Your father Abraham rejoiced that he would see my day. He saw it and was glad." So, the Jews said to him, "You are not yet fifty years old, and have you seen Abraham?" (That would have been 2,000 years before this conversation took place!)

Jesus said to them, 'Truly, truly, I say to you, before Abraham was, I AM.' They knew that this meant that Jesus was claiming to be God because look at what happens next:

"So, they picked up stones to throw at him, but Jesus hid himself and went out of the temple." They stoned people to death for blasphemy.

4. John 10:9 *"I Am the Door. If anyone enters by me, he will be saved and will go in and out and find pasture."* (Jesus is claiming that He is the one and only door that enables a person to enter and find salvation.)

5. John 10:*11 "I Am the Good Shepherd. The Good Shepherd lays down His life for the sheep."* (This was a rebuke to the religious leaders, as Jesus accused them of failing to care for the people they were meant to shepherd. In

contrast, He—God Himself—would lay down His life for His sheep, likening people to sheep.)

6. John 11:25 *"I Am the Resurrection and the Life. Whoever believes in Me, though he die, yet shall he live, and everyone who lives and believes in Me shall never die. Do you believe this?"*

7. John 14:6 *"I Am the Way, the Truth, and the Life. No one comes to the Father except through me."*

8. John 15:1 *"I Am the True Vine, and my Father is the Vinedresser."*

In all eight statements, Jesus links Himself with the God who spoke to Moses from the Burning Bush by using the title "I AM' to refer to Himself.

The "I AM" is not just a self-designating term—it is Jesus calling people to believe that He is the "I AM" of the Burning Bush—God, Yahweh.

He is calling us to come and believe in Him, because only God can save us.

Do you recognise that Jesus is God?

Obviously, many did declare their belief in Jesus. In John 8, where Jesus reveals Himself as the Light of the World, we read these words in verse 28: *"So Jesus said to them, 'When you have lifted up the Son of Man* (this was a reference to His death on the cross that was soon to take place), *then you will know that I AM, and that I do nothing on my own authority, but speak just as the Father taught me. And he who sent me is with me. He has not left me alone, for I always do the things that are pleasing to him. As he was saying these things, many believed in him."*

Yet there were many, especially the religious leaders, who did not believe that Jesus was God in the flesh, for we read in that same 8th chapter these words: *"Jesus said to them, 'If God were your Father, you would*

70

love me, for I came from God and I am here. I came not of my own accord, but he sent me. Why do you not understand what I say?"

Then Jesus answers His own question.

"It is because you cannot bear to hear my word. You are of your father the devil, and your will is to do your father's desires. He was a murderer from the beginning and does not stand in the truth because there is no truth in him. When he lies, he speaks out of his own character, for he is a liar and the father of lies. But because I tell the truth, you do not believe me." John 8:42-45.

Have you noticed that the teachings of Jesus will always draw a line in the sand, as it were, and asks:

"Will you step over from unbelief to believing and embrace Me as your Saviour and God?"

John, the writer of this Gospel, records both his personal testimony and that of John the Baptist regarding who they believed Jesus to be. "*we have seen his glory, glory as of the only Son from the Father, full of grace and truth. (John bore witness about him, and cried out, "This was he of whom I said, 'He who comes after me ranks before me, because he was before me.'") For from his fullness, we have all received, grace upon grace. For the law was given through Moses; grace and truth came through Jesus Christ. No one has ever seen God; the only God, who is at the Father's side, he has made him known.*"

I trust that as we have explored John's introduction to Jesus as God the Son, we—like John and the other believers—have seen that Jesus is truly God. *"And the Word was God."*

1. Have you Recognised?   2. Have you Believed?

3. By Receiving/Embracing?   4. Thus, Becoming a Child of God?

5.. And are you Following Him now?

Al Watson

Question Time:

Here are 10 discussion questions based on our notes: Chapter 3

1. The Deity of Jesus – John1:1 state, "The Word was with God, and the Word was God." How does this verse affirm Jesus 'divinity, and why is it essential to believe in Jesus as God for salvation?

2. Believing in His Name – The Bible teaches that salvation comes by believing in Jesus' name. How does the biblical meaning of "name" go beyond identification to include the sum total of who Jesus is?

3. Jesus as "I AM" – Jesus repeatedly used the phrase "I AM" in John's Gospel. Why did the religious leaders react so strongly to this, and how do these statements connect Jesus to the God of the Old Testament?

4. Faith and Salvation – John 8:24 states, "Unless you believe that I AM, you will die in your sins." Why is faith in Jesus 'identity as God necessary for salvation, and what does it mean to trust in Him?

5. The "I AM" Statements – Each of Jesus' eight "I AM" statements reveal something unique about His nature. Which one resonates with you most, and why?

6. Receiving Jesus – John 1:12 "says that those who believe in His name receive the right to become children of God. What does it mean to "receive" Jesus, and how is this different from simply acknowledging His existence?

7. The Role of the Holy Spirit –Recognising Jesus as God is not just an intellectual decision but a spiritual revelation. How does the Holy Spirit help people believe in and embrace Jesus?

8. The Line in the Sand – Jesus' teachings often forced people to decide about Him. What are some common reasons people struggle to step over from unbelief to belief today?

9. John's Gospel and Evangelism– John wrote his Gospel "so that you may believe" (John 20:31). How can we use the Gospel of John as a tool for sharing the message of Jesus with others?

10. Following Jesus – Recognising, believing, and receiving Jesus leads to following Him.
What does daily discipleship look like, and how can we grow in our relationship with Him?"

Al Watson

Chapter Five: Jesus the Creator

For many people, this statement is one of the most contested within our culture. Here, we discover that the Word, who is God, who became flesh and was called Jesus, is the Creator of all that exists. The God we worship is the original cause behind everything that is. John puts it this way: *"All things were made through him, and without him was not anything made that was made"* (John 1:3).

This is one area of knowledge where truth has been denied and ignored so that the forces of darkness could strengthen their grip on the minds of humanity. The Apostle Paul was spot on when he wrote to the Roman Christians: *"They exchanged the truth about God for a lie and worshiped and served the creature rather than the Creator, who is blessed forever! Amen."* (Romans 1:25).

Any young person in today's education system is presented with only one view regarding the origin of life and the causal factor behind the creation of this world. More importantly, this view is not open for debate, nor can it be challenged—despite the fact that every premise it is built on is flawed.

For hundreds of years, science believed that the world had always existed. But then, in the 1920s, we discovered that the universe has not always existed and that there was a point in time when it came into being. This led to the development of what is now known as the Big Bang theory. Then came Darwinian evolution's flawed science, with the notion that incremental changes over eons of time enabled simple life forms to become complex life forms—ultimately leading to the evolution of humankind.

How does one address this issue?

Al Watson

First, let me say that many Christians' working in scientific disciplines hold a strong commitment to the Bible's opening lines: *"In the beginning, God created the heavens and the earth"* (Genesis 1:1). These scientifically trained individuals see no contradiction between their faith in the God of the Bible and the world of true science. One such individual I know personally is Professor John C. Lennox, PhD, DPhil, DSc, who is Professor of Mathematics (Emeritus) at the University of Oxford. Dr. Lennox has engaged in several debates with Dr. Richard Dawkins, which can be found on YouTube.

Anyone can have an opinion, but you cannot have your own opinion on the facts. Almost everything that supports Darwinian evolution is based on opinions rather than measurable or testable scientific facts.

Ignoring facts while reaching conclusions results in erroneous conclusions.

Scripture has never claimed to be a scientific book, but it will never contradict true science. When you consider what the Bible says about the creation of the world, its statements are simple, clear, and beyond contradiction. Genesis 1:1 state, "In the beginning, God created." There was a beginning. Was it a single Big Bang or multiple Big Bangs as God spoke events into existence? We know that "nothing" cannot create "something." Even the evolutionist must answer where that "something" originated before it could go Bang!

We have no idea how God did it, but we know that He is the only logical explanation for the origin of the Earth and the vast array of stars and planets surrounding us. Everything points to intelligent design. *"And God said, 'Let there be,' and there was."* In other words, every first creation was spoken into existence. There was no gradual evolutionary development—God simply spoke, and it came to be. From that moment on, creatures reproduced *"after their own kind,"* meaning within their species. To this day, species cannot crossbreed to create new species. Even animals that appear similar, like horses and donkeys, can produce offspring, but those offspring (mules) are sterile and cannot reproduce further.

Identity

However, animals can develop within their own species. For example, I have experience with cattle (bovines). Through selective breeding, the size of an animal can change over time. You can have a Lowline bull weighing around 350 kilograms or a large Angus bull weighing 1,300 kilograms. Both belong to the same species—Angus cattle. The difference is simply the result of selective breeding for size and weight.

The Bible is factually correct: species can only reproduce within their own species, or as the Bible puts it, "after their kind."

Having grandchildren in the education system, I purchased the Year 10 textbook used in their curriculum to understand how the education system presents its alternative to the Bible's account. The textbook was Pearson Science SB, 2nd Edition 10.

On page 156, under "The Evidence for Evolution", five sources were presented. The textbook states:

"There is now so much evidence for the theory of evolution by natural selection that very few scientists doubt its validity. The sources of the evidence are mainly in five areas:"

1. The fossil record
2. Comparative anatomy
3. Genetics and biochemistry
4. Geographic distribution of species
5. Embryology

If you examine these points individually, many unanswered questions arise—questions that should lead us to critically assess the conclusions presented in the textbook.

"That very few scientists doubt its validity."

This statement is highly questionable because many scientists would disagree. How many scientists worldwide have been surveyed regarding their stance on Darwinian evolution? Moreover, what makes one scientist's opinion more valuable than another? This is not solely a scientific issue—it is influenced by a scientist's worldview and academic training. If only one worldview is taught, and the logical flow of evidence is structured to support that view, with few willing or able to challenge it, then it is only a matter of time before a theory is treated as if it were a fact.

The Fossil Record

The textbook presents the standard argument that simpler life forms are found in lower layers of the Earth's surface, while more complex life forms appear in higher rock strata. This is known as the geological time scale. However, two key questions remain unanswered:

Where can we find a clear example of the geological time scale? Reports I have seen show mixtures of many species from different supposed time periods within the same fossil layer, suggesting they existed simultaneously. If that is the case, how can it be stated that simpler life forms are always found in lower layers while more complex ones appear higher up? There is nowhere in the world where such an uninterrupted geological time scale actually exists as described. Except on the pages of School text books.

How do evolutionists explain the formation of so many preserved fossils? In real-life conditions, animals that die are typically consumed by scavengers and decompose long before fossilisation can occur. The sheer number of well-preserved fossils suggests that they must have been buried rapidly under massive layers of sediment. This aligns with the idea of a catastrophic flood, such as Noah's flood, which could have buried vast numbers of animals under mountains of debris—leading to their preservation in skeletal form.

Comparative Anatomy

This field examines the skeletal structures of animals to identify similarities. The textbook illustrates how whales, bats, monkeys, pigs, and horses all have limb structures resembling the human arm and hand. At first glance, these drawings suggest a commonality.

However, the conclusion drawn from this observation is where the debate begins. Darwinian evolution argues that one species gradually evolved into another, with skeletal structures adapting to suit the needs of the developing species.

But there is another explanation, which is equally valid. A simple analogy can help clarify this: Imagine walking down a street and observing the houses. While they vary in appearance, they share common features—walls, windows, doors, and roofs. Why? Because a functional house requires these elements. The same principle applies to living creatures. Their skeletal structures were designed for their specific functions from the very beginning. When God spoke them into existence, they were already fully formed—and they have remained the same ever since.

The textbook also presents Darwin's study of finches on the Galápagos Islands, highlighting how those with stronger, larger beaks survived, while finches with smaller, weaker beaks died out. Two important observations should be noted:

1. The finches remained finches—even as beak sizes changed, they did not evolve into a different species.
2. Mutations within their DNA—resulting from genetic degeneration—led to some finches developing larger, stronger beaks. Since the available seeds were hard-shelled, these finches survived, while those with smaller beaks perished.

If one wants to refer to this as natural selection, that is fine—because the same principle applies to selective breeding in cattle, as discussed earlier. The key difference is that humans controlled the selection process in cattle, whereas nature determined which finches survived based on their beak strength.

However, this process does not support cross-species evolution. The finches remained finches, just as God decreed that species would only reproduce within their own kind. This is not just a theological claim—it is a scientific fact.

Genetics and Biochemistry

The textbook begins with an outrageous statement:

"Although scientists knew that similarities between organisms *were evidence of a shared ancestry*, they did not know how these characteristics were passed on." (Emphasis added)

This claim is purely speculative, as there is no concrete evidence for shared ancestry. In fact, the very DNA that this textbook presents as "recently discovered proof of shared ancestry" demonstrates the exact opposite.

The human body contains cells, and within those cells is DNA—a blueprint that dictates how each cell structures itself. As cells multiply, they retain and pass on identical genetic information. The widely cited claim that humans and chimpanzees share 96% genetic similarity was made long before the discovery of DNA. Now that we can properly analyse DNA, we know the actual similarity is closer to 70%.

There are similarities because both species require similar biological structures—a skeleton, arms, legs, eyes, ears, skin, teeth, fingers, and so on. This is no different from the similarities found in houses—all homes share common features because they require the same basic components to function properly.

Additionally, the percentage of genetic similarity remains highly debated. But even if we accept (which we do not) the 96% similarity figure, the remaining 4% difference translates to over 35 million bits of information! The original claim of 96% was made before scientists had the tools to fully analyse genetic structures. Yet, the textbook presents this claim as fact, despite it having no measurable scientific basis.

Identity

Geographic Distribution of Species

This argument is simple: when species become isolated on islands, they adapt to their environment. However, the textbook makes a false claim:

"If isolation lasts for a long period of time, then the different populations eventually become different species."

This is misleading. In the real world, species cannot and do not change into different species. One species cannot transform into another. While certain characteristics may change over time, the species itself remains the same—which is why isolated species are still able to reproduce within their own kind, and with all species from other locations around the world.

The textbook tries to prove their point with the illustration using finches on the Galápagos Islands, stating that some developed bigger beaks while others had smaller beaks. But as we have already established, they were still finches—they did not evolve into magpies or any other bird species.

Embryology

This argument is especially frustrating. The textbook includes pictures of embryos from six different species and suggests that because they appear to have tails at an early stage, all species must have evolved from an ancestor with a tail—such as a fish.

The textbook claims:

"Biologists long ago proposed that fish evolved into amphibians, which evolved into reptiles, which evolved into birds."

This conclusion is drawn simply by observing similarities in embryos—yet this logic is deeply flawed. For example, what some scientists call a tail in a human embryo four weeks after conception actually develops into legs. The presence of similar embryonic structures does not prove an evolutionary link.

A simple analogy demonstrates the flaw in this reasoning: Imagine looking at the foundations of multiple buildings before they are constructed. At this stage, you would have no idea what the finished buildings will look like. However, all buildings require a foundation and will share some similarities in their early construction phase. That does not mean one building evolved into another—it simply means they were designed using similar architectural principles.

The Underlying Issue: Science or Philosophy?

This brings us to a crucial point: Why do these misleading conclusions persist?

The answer is philosophy, not science. The first premise of modern scientific thought is that the material world is the only real world. This worldview assumes that everything in existence is governed solely by natural laws and that humanity—being a product of this material world—must submit to these laws.

Under this framework, God cannot exist because He is not material and cannot be observed. Therefore, He is dismissed outright.

This is why Paul told the Christians in Corinth:

"The natural person does not accept the things of the Spirit of God, for they are folly to him, and he is not able to understand them because they are spiritually discerned." (1 Corinthians 2:14)

And why he warned the believers in Rome:

"For the wrath of God is revealed from heaven against all ungodliness and unrighteousness of men, who by their unrighteousness suppress the truth. For what can be known about God is plain to them, because God has shown it to them. For his invisible attributes, namely, his eternal power and divine nature, have been clearly

perceived, ever since the creation of the world, in the things that have been made. So they are without excuse. For although they knew God, they did not honour him as God or give thanks to him, but they became futile in their thinking, and their foolish hearts were darkened. Claiming to be wise, they became fools, and exchanged the glory of the immortal God for images resembling mortal man and birds and animals and creeping things." (Romans 1:18-23)

And in today's world, the one true God has been explained away in the name of so-called superior wisdom. As this passage points out all mankind should at least honour God as the Great Creator. But *"became fools, and exchanged the glory of the immortal God for images resembling mortal man"*.

Final Thoughts

The issue we face is not about finding convincing proof to persuade non-believers that "In the beginning, God created." As John reminds us, speaking of Jesus: *"All things were made by Him, and without Him nothing was made that is made."*

The Holy Spirit has the final word on the question, "Where did we come from?" His answer is recorded in Hebrews 11:3: *"By faith we understand that the universe was created by the word of God, so that what is seen was not made out of things that are visible."*

The greatest scientists in the world were not there when creation happened. They can only examine what they believe to be evidence. However, because they cannot conceive of the God of the Bible as real, they have constructed a narrative that they blindly accept as an explanation for the origin of life.

But when God is brought into the equation, the same evidence takes on an entirely different—and far more honest—perspective on what we call facts.

Al Watson

Here are 10 questions based on our notes: Chapter 5

1. According to John 1:3, what role did Jesus (the Word) play in creation, and how does this challenge modern scientific assumptions about the origin of life?

2. How does Romans 1:25 help explain the cultural shift from worshipping the Creator to worshipping created things?

3. What major shift occurred in scientific thinking about the universe in the 1920s, and how did it impact theories about the beginning of life?

4. How does Professor John Lennox represent the compatibility between Christian faith and science?
Why is this significant in the debate over origins?

5. What is the biblical explanation for species development, and how does it differ from the theory of Darwinian evolution?

6. Why does the author challenge the five pieces of evidence for evolution found in the Year 10 science textbook? Provide one example of a counterpoint raised in the lecture.

7. In what ways does the fossil record present difficulties for the evolutionary timeline? How might a biblical flood account provide an alternative explanation?

8. How does the example of the Galápagos finches illustrate the difference between natural selection and evolution into a new species?

Identity

9. What is the key flaw in using embryology to support the idea of a common ancestor, according to the lecture?

10. The final section argues that the debate over origins is more about philosophy than science. What

worldview assumptions influence how scientists interpret evidence, and how does Romans 1:18–23 describe the result of suppressing the truth about God?

Al Watson

Chapter Six: Jesus the Life

John reveals that Jesus the Word was Life. *"In him was life."* John 1:4 Throughout the gospel of John, the word life, always refers to spiritual life, eternal life, new life and this life is the life that Jesus creates *"and this is the testimony God has given us eternal life and this life is in his Son. He who has the Son has life, he who does not have the Son of God does not have life."* (1. John 5: 11–12)

Every living thing—whether plant, animal, or human—comes from pre-existing life. As we saw in our last chapter, some propose that life is the result of natural selection, where mutations have gradually developed higher forms over vast periods of time, science has never been able to explain the origin of life itself. We may understand much about how life functions, but we have little to no understanding of what it is and how it begins.

As Scripture declares: *"All things were made by Him, and without Him, nothing was made that has been made."* (John 1:3) Jesus not only created all things—He is the One who gives life. We live because Jesus IS Life!

However, when John said, *"In Him was life, and the life was the light of men"* (John 1:4), he was not referring to physical life but to spiritual life. We know this because every time John speaks of *life*, it is within the context of spiritual life.

Jesus came that mankind *"might have life, and have it more abundantly"* (John 10:10). He died so that men might *"have everlasting life"* (John 3:16). It is His life that keeps men from perishing: *"I give them eternal life, and they will never perish, and no one will snatch them out of my hand"* (John 10:28).

While the ultimate source of life is the Father, *"For as the Father has life in Himself, so He has granted the Son also to have life in Himself"* (John 5:26). This is the life that can give our dead spirits LIFE.

Physically, we may be alive, but without Christ, we are spiritually dead. Paul reminds the believers of this reality in Ephesians:

"And you were dead in the trespasses and sins in which you once walked, following the course of this world, following the prince of the power of the air, the spirit that is now at work in the sons of disobedience— among whom we all once lived in the passions of our flesh, carrying out the desires of the body and the mind, and were by nature children of wrath, like the rest of mankind." (Ephesians 2:1-3)

Notice that Paul uses the past tense—*"were dead"*—because, in Christ, spiritual death is replaced with new life. The spirit that was once dead can now be alive:

"But God, being rich in mercy, because of the great love with which He loved us, even when we were dead in our trespasses, made us alive together with Christ—by grace you have been saved." (Ephesians 2:4-5) Through Christ, a believer is no longer spiritually dead but alive in Him.

This raises the question, What Does It Mean to Be Spiritually Dead?

When something dies, the life that once animated it ceases to exist. Something that is dead has no sensation of loss, no lingering memory. But, if you were to lose an arm after years of living with it, you would be acutely aware of its absence.

Similarly, within every human being is a God-shaped void—a longing for the presence of the One who is no longer there. When Adam disobeyed God and ate from the forbidden tree, he experienced death. This was not immediate physical death, but spiritual death was instant. His connection to the source of life was severed.

Identity

Since that moment, all of humanity has carried an echo of that loss. When people worship, pray, or seek to understand God, they are responding to this deep, inherent awareness of separation—a longing to restore what was lost.

To help us grasp spiritual death, Jesus gave us a powerful illustration. He allowed a friend, Lazarus, to die— demonstrating our spiritual state. Just as Lazarus was physically dead, we, too, are spiritually dead because we were born that way with a sin nature.

Lazarus lay in a tomb; our dead spirit remains within us. A dead body has no desires, no understanding, no sensitivity, no longing—because it is lifeless. Likewise, a spiritually dead person has no desires, no understanding, no sensitivity, no longing, no true hunger for God, no capacity to reach for Him, no spiritual life within.

Yet, when Jesus stood before Lazarus's grave and called him back to life, a new creation took place. Lazarus emerged from the tomb, fully alive, experiencing all the realities of life once again—until the day for the second time he died physically.

This miracle of Lazarus mirrors the transformation that occurs when Christ calls our dead spirit to life. Only He has the power to resurrect not just the body, but the spirit—restoring us to the life we were meant to have in Him.

It was the call of Jesus that brought Lazarus back to life, and as Paul, speaking about where we find faith, says in Romans 10:17, "*So faith comes from hearing, and hearing through the word of Christ.*" Our dead lifeless spirits are made alive only when we hear the voice of Jesus. Or, to use another metaphor that Paul uses ".. God, who said, "Let light shine out of darkness," has shone in our hearts to give the light of the knowledge of the glory of God in the face of Jesus Christ." 2 Corinthians 4:6. This can be our experience

when we place our faith in Him—trusting in God's forgiveness, which removes the penalty of sin we once faced through Jesus' sacrifice on the

A New Creation

Paul describes those who receive spiritual life through faith in Jesus as *"new creations"*:

"Therefore, if anyone is in Christ, the new creation has come: The old has gone, the new is here! All this

is from God..." (2 Corinthians 5:17-18).

By calling the born-again believer a *new creation*, Paul draws a direct connection to Genesis and the creation narrative. The similarities are striking:

Creation begins in darkness, and then God creates light—*"The evening and the morning were the first day."* (Genesis 1:5). Darkness comes first, then light.

This raises a point of contention, as the sun—the primary source of our light—was not created until the fourth day. However, Scripture reminds us that God Himself is Light: *"God is Light, and in Him is no darkness at all."* (1 John 1:5). For those first three days Gods light became the prototype for the sun, moon and stars.

There is no need to rearrange the days of creation. The seven days are clearly recorded, each structured the same way—*evening and morning, darkness then light*. I believe this is intentional, illustrating the Gospel of Jesus Christ. The entire Old Testament is about Jesus, and if we lose sight of that, we will fail to understand its message (Luke 24:25-27, 44-45). Creations order illustrates mankind's spiritual state because of sin.

2. Spiritual blindness and the need for divine illumination.

"The god of this age has blinded the minds of unbelievers, so that they cannot see the light of the gospel that displays the glory of Christ, who is the image of God." 2 Corinthians 4:4.

We are all born into darkness. Then, as we have already pointed out, in verse 6 we read *"For God who said, "Let light shine out of darkness", has shone in our hearts to give the light of the knowledge of the glory of God in the face of Jesus Christ."* So, for the light of understanding to come to any person requires a work of God. Notice that "God reveals the Light of the Glory of God in the face of Jesus"

Just as God spoke physical light into existence, He must bring spiritual light into the heart of a person. This is a divine work, not something we can achieve on our own. Notice that Paul emphasises *"God reveals the light of His glory in the face of Jesus."* This is why the Gospel is all about knowing Christ. A person embraces Jesus when their eyes are opened to who He truly is.

A perfect illustration of this is Peter's encounter with Jesus in Luke 5:1-11 Peter, and his fellow fishermen had worked all night without success. Then Jesus commanded him to launch into the deep and let down the nets. To Peter as a seasoned fisherman, this seemed completely irrational—in daylight, fish would see the nets and avoid them. Yet Peter obeyed:

"But because You say so, I will let down the nets." (Luke 5:5).

After catching an overwhelming number of fish, Peter suddenly realised who Jesus truly was—and, in turn, recognised his own sinfulness. He fell at Jesus' feet, saying:

"Depart from me, for I am a sinful man, O Lord." (Luke 5:8).

When God shines the truth of the Gospel into a person's heart, they do not merely gain knowledge or information; they see Jesus for who He is and recognise their own sin. This is an act of God, not human reaction.

Spiritual Birth: A Work of God

John 1:12-13 makes it abundantly clear that salvation is God's work, not ours:

"But to all who did receive Him, who believed in His name, He gave the right to become children of God—

who were born, not of blood *(not through family lineage)*, nor of the will of the flesh *(not by human effort)*, nor of the will of man *(not through religious rituals or the decision of others)*, but of God."*(Emphasis added)*

Just as we had nothing to do with our physical birth, we are not the creators of our spiritual birth. It is entirely God's work.

Through Jesus, God entered our world to bring light into our darkness, life into our spiritual death, and hope into our hopelessness.

Light Comes When God Speaks

At creation, God's command brought forth physical light. In the new birth, light comes through His Word—specifically, the Gospel of Jesus Christ. As John presents in his Gospel, understanding and spiritual awakening come through a work of God.

This is why Jesus sent His followers into the world to proclaim the Gospel, empowering them to do so: *"But you will receive power when the Holy Spirit has come upon you, and you will be my witnesses in Jerusalem and in all Judea and Samaria, and to the end of the earth."* (Acts 1:8)

Paul reinforces this necessity in Romans 10:14: *"How shall they hear without a preacher?"*

In other words, the message must be spoken. Without words, people will not hear. Unfortunately, some have adopted the saying:

"Preach the Gospel, and if necessary, use words."

If that is your thinking—get rid of it. The only way people will hear the Gospel is if someone proclaims it, tells it, teaches it. God has chosen to use our witness as the means of revealing Christ to the world. We could use any conversion in the New Testament to illustrate this. A key example of is the conversion of Lydia in Acts 16:14. Paul preached, and:

"The Lord opened her heart to pay attention to what was said by Paul."

This pattern is seen throughout Scripture and life—people come to faith through the spoken Word. The Gospel must be declared for the light of Christ to shine in people's hearts.

In Creation, when God gave life to Adam, He imparted His own breath of life, and man became alive. In the New Creation, it is also the life of Jesus that grants us new life. His life dwells within us:

"And this is the testimony: God has given us eternal life, and this life is in His Son. He who has the Son has life; he who does not have the Son of God does not have life." — 1 John 5:11–12.

"Very truly I tell you, whoever hears my word and believes Him who sent me has eternal life and will not be judged but has crossed over from death to life." — John 5:24.

"Very truly I tell you, a time is coming and has now come when the dead will hear the voice of the Son of God, and those who hear will live." — John 5:25.

No wonder Paul declared:

Al Watson

"Christ in you, the hope of glory." — Colossians 1:27

There is a living, walking, rejoicing, and creative person as a result of the spiritual life that God gives. Before receiving that breath of life, there was only a lifeless body—incapable of action, without desires, strength, reason, sight, smell, taste, or sensitivity. Adam was nothing more than a lifeless form, equivalent to a dead corpse. But the life given by God changed everything—Adam became fully alive in every sense.

The same is true for anyone born of the Spirit of God. They exhibit all the characteristics of a spiritually alive person, reflecting the transformation that comes through His life within them.

So, what does that look like when The Word/Jesus gives us His Life to indwell us?

You begin your journey as a newborn believer and follower of Christ, just as all babies crave and need milk. "As newborn babes, desire the sincere milk of the word, that you may grow thereby: If you have tasted that the Lord is gracious." — 1 Peter 2:2-3 (KJV)

Your faith cannot be separated from the Bible. Jesus Himself said:

"Man shall not live by bread alone, but by every word that comes from the mouth of God." — Matthew 4:4 John not only wrote the Gospel but also three short letters to Christians and recorded the book of Revelation as Jesus revealed it to him. In *1 John*, we find key characteristics of the life of Jesus within a believer.

For example, John states: "No one who is born of God will continue to sin, because God's seed remains in him; he cannot go on sinning, because he has been born of God." — 1 John 3:9

The phrases *"continue to sin"* and *"he cannot go on sinning"* convey the idea of habitually living the same way as before coming to Christ. While you still live in an old body, the new life within you will take control. If you do sin, you will quickly become aware of it because the Holy Spirit, who dwells within you, will convict you. This conviction is often realized through a sense of guilt, but God's grace provides a way forward:

"If we confess our sins, He is faithful and just to forgive us our sins, and to cleanse us from all unrighteousness." — 1 John 1:9 John further affirms:

"If you know that He (Jesus) is righteous, you may be sure that everyone who practices righteousness has been born of Him." — 1 John 2:29

Christlike love will naturally emerge in your behaviour.

"Beloved, let us love one another, for love is from God, and whoever loves has been born of God and knows God. Anyone who does not love does not know God, because God is love." — 1 John 4:7-8

It is important to remember that love is a verb—an action, not just a feeling. John reminds us:

"But if anyone has the world's goods and sees his brother in need, yet closes his heart against him, how does God's love abide in him? Little children, let us not love in word or talk but in deed and in truth." — 1 John 3:17-18

True love is demonstrated through action, reflecting the very nature of God in how we care for and serve others.

While we now live by a new set of values, the people of this world, as the saying goes, march to the beat of a different drum. However, the new life within us no longer gives in to the aspirations of this world.

John affirms this truth:

"For everyone who has been born of God overcomes the world. And this is the victory that has overcome the world—our faith. Who is it that overcomes the world except the one who believes that Jesus is the Son of God?" — 1 John 5:4-5

Through faith in Christ, we are no longer bound by worldly desires but are empowered to live victoriously in alignment with His will.

At times, the temptation and pressure of this world can feel overwhelming—so much so that it seems as if there is more than just human influence at work, urging us to conform or to do wrong. John reassures us:

"We know that everyone who has been born of God does not keep on sinning, but He who was born of God (Jesus) protects him, and the evil one does not touch him.

We know that we are from God, and the whole world lies in the power of the evil one.

And we know that the Son of God has come and has given us understanding, so that we may know Him who is true; and we are in Him who is true, in His Son Jesus Christ. He is the true God and eternal life." — 1 John 5:18-20

Jesus is the author and giver of life, and that life within us naturally produces behaviour that reflects our Heavenly Father. As Jesus said, people should see our good works and glorify our Father in heaven. He also declared, *"By their fruits you will know them."*

If you wonder what kind of fruit an authentic Christ-follower displays, Paul provides the answer:

"But the fruit of the Spirit is love, joy, peace, patience, kindness, goodness, faithfulness, gentleness, self- control; against such things there is no law. And those who belong to Christ Jesus have crucified the flesh with its passions and desires. If we live by the Spirit, let us also keep in step with the Spirit." — Galatians 5:22-25.

You can only live the life that pulses within you, and for the Christ-follower, that is life of Jesus!

Identity

Question Time:

Here are 10 questions based on our notes: Chapter 6.

1. **Jesus as the Source of Life** – John 1:4 states, "In Him was life, and the life was the light of men." How does this verse distinguish between physical life and spiritual life?

2. **Spiritual Death and New Life** – Ephesians 2:1-5 describes humanity as being spiritually dead before Christ gives us life. How does the story of Lazarus illustrate this transformation?

3. **God-Shaped Void** – Your notes mention that every human has an innate longing for God due to spiritual death. How does this longing manifest in people's lives, and what are some common ways people try to fill it apart from Christ?

4. **Hearing and Responding to the Gospel** – Romans 10:17 states that "faith comes by hearing, and hearing through the word of Christ." How does this emphasize the necessity of proclaiming the Gospel with words rather than just actions?

5. **The Role of Light in Salvation** – 2 Corinthians 4:6 speaks of God shining light into the hearts of believers. What does this reveal about the process of salvation and the role of divine revelation?

6. **Spiritual Birth as a Divine Work** – John 1:12-13 makes it clear that becoming a child of God is not by human effort but by God's will. How does this challenge the idea that we can earn salvation through good works?

7. **Transformation in Christ** – 2 Corinthians 5:17 states that those in Christ are a "new creation." How does this transformation impact a believer's daily life and choices?

8. **Evidence of a Changed Life** – 1 John 3:9 says that those born of God do not continue in habitual sin. How does this passage relate to the ongoing process of sanctification in a believer's life?

9. **Overcoming the World** – 1 John 5:4-5 declares that those born of God overcome the world through faith. What are some practical ways believers can resist worldly influences while living in a secular culture?

10. **The Fruit of the Spirit** – Galatians 5:22-25 outlines characteristics that should be evident in a believer's life. How does the presence (or absence) of these qualities indicate the depth of someone's relationship with Christ?

Identity

Chapter Seven: Jesus is the Light

Light is used as a metaphor to contrast God and Satan, good and evil, light and darkness. Light represents all that is of God, and darkness represents all that opposes God.

In verse 4, it is the life of Jesus that is the light: "*In Him was life, and that life was the light of men.*"

Notice that it is the life of Jesus that gives light to mankind. Also, notice that this light shines into the darkness.

There is a change of tense here. The first four verses speak of things in the past—for example, the words "was" or "were" are used eight times. Now we have the word "shines," meaning the light is "continually in action."

Where does this light shine?

The light shines in the darkness—and remember that darkness represents all that is opposed to God—and the darkness could not "what"?

This Greek word, which the ESV has translated as "not overcome it" and the NIV has translated as "has not understood it," also has a reading in the margin as "overpowered it."

Whatever the response of darkness is, remember the light does what it always does—it shines. And when it shines, by its very nature, it dispels the darkness.

How great a removal of darkness occurs depends on the strength of the light shining. There is a great difference between the strength of the sun and that of a candle.

The light that is Jesus shines, and darkness has no power over it. But it is obvious that, in this case, darkness seeks to flee from the light of Jesus.

In John 3:19-20, he points out: *"Light has come into the world, but people loved darkness instead of light because their deeds were evil. Everyone who does evil hates the light and will not come into the light for fear that their deeds will be exposed."*

What are we to learn from this?

In this world of darkness, Christ-followers are responsible for continuing to shine the light of the life of Jesus into the darkness, even if this darkened world will never welcome it, seek to know it, or embrace it—unless something supernatural occurs.

This then begs the question: How will anyone come to the "Light"?

This is best answered by reading Paul's experience at Corinth. He faced great opposition as he preached that Jesus was the Messiah.

Then, *"One night the Lord spoke to Paul in a vision: 'Do not be afraid; keep on speaking, do not be silent. For I am with you, and no one is going to attack and harm you, because I have many people in this city.'*

So, Paul stayed in Corinth for a year and a half, teaching them the word of God." (Acts 18:9-11).

Later, Paul wrote to the Christ-followers at Corinth and reminded them of what had taken place in their lives. Once, they were in their darkness and facing destruction because *"the god of this age had blinded the minds of unbelievers, so that they cannot see the light of the gospel that displays the glory of*

Christ, who is the image of God." Then, Paul reminded them that he preached *"…Jesus Christ as Lord."*

So how did the light that is Jesus overcome the darkness?

"For God, who said, 'Let light shine out of darkness'" (this was speaking of the events in Genesis chapter one, where there was only darkness, and God spoke, "Let there be light," and there was light).

Light of understanding comes when God speaks. It wasn't only Paul who was speaking God dispelled the darkness.

And He will speak through His people who take the message of the Gospel into the world of darkness. This is what Paul did: *"'Do not be afraid,'(God said), 'keep on speaking, do not be silent… I have many people in this city.' So, Paul stayed in Corinth for a year and a half, teaching them the word of God."*

When people are not the slightest bit interested in the Gospel, God, who makes His light shine in hearts to give *"the light of the knowledge of God's glory displayed in the face of Christ,"* will remove blind eyes, change hardened hearts, and give the gift of faith.

People are then keen to embrace Jesus as their Saviour. You only have to look at the conversion of the Apostle Paul (Acts 9) as an example of the power of God in bringing light into a person's life. I think it is fair to say that Saul/Paul did not leave for Damascus that morning thinking, "Well, today will be a good day to become a believer and follower of Jesus the Messiah."

What God did to Saul/Paul, He will do for all who take those steps to *"call upon His name."* He will overcome the greatest resistance—even when people have no desire to call upon the Lord and be saved.

One of the best illustrations of the process that God uses to bring people *"…from the dominion of darkness*

....*into the kingdom of the Son he loves...*" (Colossians 1:13) is the parable of the Sower in Luke 8:4-15.

The picture would have been a common sight to people in the Middle East at the time of Jesus. A farmer had a bag of seed over his shoulder, and as he walked along the ploughed field, he threw handfuls of seed onto the ground. Jesus takes this mental picture and presents the Gospel's power in action.

You have the seed, the sower, and the soil in this parable, and each of these three carries a message.

The Seed is the "Word of God," and there is no limitation to its power to reproduce life. Again, the seed

is more than just a message—the seed is the message about Jesus. As Jesus said in John 12:24, "*Very truly I tell you, unless a kernel of wheat falls to the ground and dies, it remains only a single seed. But if it dies, it produces many seeds.*" Jesus likened Himself to that grain of wheat that fell into the ground and died.

The death was the cross, and it was through that dying that He has the power to produce many "seeds," which represent His followers.

Therefore, Paul made that bold statement: "*The Gospel is the power of God unto salvation to everyone who believes...*" (Romans 1:16).

But the message of the Gospel is only the means of introducing people to Jesus, for it is only when we believe and receive Him by faith that all that Jesus can bring to a person's life will take effect.

The Sower represents the followers of Jesus—the people who, for generations, have fulfilled the Lord's commission: "*...go and make disciples of all nations, baptising them in the name of the Father and of the Son and of the Holy Spirit, and teaching them to obey everything I have commanded you. And surely, I am with you always, to the very end of the age.*" (Matthew 28:19-20).

Here, Christ-followers need to personalise Paul's instruction to his fellow worker Timothy:

"For this reason, I remind you to fan into flame the gift of God, which is in you through the laying on of my hands. For the Spirit God gave us does not make us timid, but gives us power, love, and self-discipline. So, do not be ashamed of the testimony about our Lord or of me, his prisoner. Rather, join with me in suffering for the Gospel, by the power of God." (2 Timothy 1:6-8).

Paul continues *"But you, keep your head in all situations, endure hardship, do the work of an evangelist, discharge all the duties of your ministry."* (2 Timothy 4:5).

Evangelism is a job or a task rather than a gift. We all have the privilege of partnering with the Holy Spirit in this ministry. Also, remember what Paul told the Corinthian Christians:

"I planted the seed, Apollos watered it, but God has been making it grow." (1 Corinthians 3:6).

In Jesus parable, the soils represent the hearts of people who hear the Gospel. The condition of the soil when the seed was sown represents the competitive forces of the "kingdom of darkness," for we find some soils— or hearts—hard, shallow, and committed to other priorities.

Then there is the good soil, which is receptive and reproduces the character of the seed that was sown.

We take this to mean that it is only those who have the seed—which is the life of Jesus within them—who become Christ-followers.

You have two groups here: Professors and Possessors. Or, as Hebrews 6:4-6 says:

"It is impossible for those who have once been enlightened, who have tasted the heavenly gift, who have shared in the Holy Spirit, who have tasted the goodness of the word of God and the powers of the coming age and who have fallen away, to be

brought back to repentance. To their loss, they are crucifying the Son of God all over again and subjecting him to public disgrace."

These words describe the experience of Judas, who, for three years, walked with Jesus as a disciple. Thankfully, we know that Paul clearly stated to Timothy: *"...God's firm foundation stands, bearing this seal: 'The Lord knows those who are his,'* (and by implication, we don't), *and, 'Let everyone who names the name of the Lord depart from iniquity.'"*

The nearest we come to knowing who the Christ-followers are is by their changed lifestyles. Considering this passage, let's look at the soil types.

The First Soil Type

The first soil type was the hard pathway where people walked. This was so hard that the seed just lay on the ground, was trampled on, and the birds came to remove it.

Jesus interprets this by saying:

"Those along the path are the ones who hear, and then the devil comes and takes away the word from their hearts, so that they may not believe and be saved."

So how does the Devil take away the seed sown?

He employs many ways. Think of distractions—you hear a message, but then you remember that you have an appointment with a friend, or you recall that your favourite TV show is on tonight. The list is as varied as people are different.

The Devil and his forces find it simple to bring a competitive thought into our minds, and they are masters at doing this.

Or what about reason and educated training?

In a secular, educated world, the notion of Jesus, the cross, the death and resurrection of the dead, and even the idea that there is a God runs countercultural to our educated minds. It's easy to bring learned arguments to our minds that lead us to dismiss the truth of Jesus being God, our Saviour.

Darkened minds are often very dark, and like many, they *"receive not the things of the Spirit of God"—they are foolishness to them, and they cannot understand them* (1 Corinthians 2:14).

But remember, the Church is filled with many Gospel-hardened people who are now brothers and sisters in the Kingdom of God, because the God who said "Let there be light" at the beginning of creation has caused the Gospel to shine into their lives, showing them the love, beauty, and glory of Christ, who is now their Saviour, Lord, and hope of glory.

These people now praise God for the gift of faith. It is the truth that sets people free, and that is the only message we have.

Hosea, the Old Testament prophet, spoke about breaking up the fallow ground—that is, the hard, impregnable hearts of his audience:

"Sow to yourselves in righteousness, reap in mercy; break up your fallow ground: for it is time to seek the Lord, till he come and rain righteousness upon you." (Hosea 10:12)

When we speak the truth in love, sometimes it creates "the stone in the shoe syndrome," where the message troubles you.

It was God who said:

"So is my word that goes out from my mouth: It will not return to me empty but will accomplish what I desire and achieve the purpose for which I sent it." (Isaiah 55:11)

That is why Peter said people will be born again from imperishable seed, which is the living and enduring word of God (1 Peter 1:23). Share the truth with people even when they are reluctant to hear or accept it.

The Rocky Ground

The seed sown on rocky ground is not talking about soil mixed with rocks but soil that lies on top of large rocks underneath, making the layer of soil very shallow. Therefore, the soil has no ability to hold moisture within its structure.

This means that while the seed sprouted, it soon died in the heat of the sun because it had no moisture to sustain life. All plants need the sun, but without moisture to sustain life, the plants die.

Jesus looks at this and applies the illustration to people who receive the message with joy. In other words, they had enough understanding of the Gospel and wanted to believe it. People can understand the teaching of the Gospel in their minds and intellectually believe it.

Romans tells us:

"Since what may be known about God is plain to them, because God has made it plain to them. For since the creation of the world God's invisible qualities—his eternal power and divine nature—have been clearly seen, being understood from what has been made, so that people are without excuse. For although they knew God, they neither glorified him as God nor gave thanks to him, but their thinking became futile, and their foolish hearts were darkened." (Romans 1:19-21)

But faith is more than mere intellectual assent. Jesus said these people had no root—that is, a very shallow understanding of the truths of the Gospel. When times of testing came, such as intellectual arguments against faith, persecution, or the moral demands of conformity to behaviour that reflects one's faith, these professors "fell away."

They were lost, and their faith was not real, Christ-indwelling faith. These professors were not possessors.

Notice that it was because they had no roots that they fell away. This simply means that we need to go deep into God through His Word. Look how Paul prayed for the Christians in Ephesus:

"For this reason, I kneel before the Father, from whom every family in heaven and on earth derives its name. I pray that out of his glorious riches he may strengthen you with power through his Spirit in your inner being, so that Christ may dwell in your hearts through faith. And I pray that you, being rooted and established in love, may have power, together with all the Lord's holy people, to grasp how wide and long and high and deep is the love of Christ, and to know this love that surpasses knowledge— that you may be filled to the measure of all the fullness of God. Now to him who is able to do immeasurably more than all we ask or imagine, according to his power that is at work within us, to him be glory in the church and in Christ Jesus throughout all generations, for ever and ever! Amen." (Ephesians 3:14-21)

The Thorny Soil

The next soil is good in the sense that the seed germinated and started to grow. But the problem was that the soil was filled with competing interests. These are described as "other seeds" like thorns or weeds, which choked the life out of the plant that had sprouted.

Competing Interests

Jesus interprets the weeds to be three competing interests in one's faith:

- Worries in this life
    - Riches
    - Pleasures

Faith is about trusting the person you have placed your faith in. Everyone will face hard times, but during those hard times, we need to ask ourselves: Is my God able to provide, protect, guide, heal, restore?

The answer is often shaped by our own expectations of what God's help should look like.

For example: "Lord, I have cancer. Please heal me." But nothing happens—the cancer is still there and getting worse. So where is God? He hasn't healed.

The truth is, God always heals. He may take the cancer from you, and you live, or He might take you from the cancer, and you go to be with the Lord. It's a win-win, no matter what.

God has healed—but has He done it the way you want?

Do you trust Him to the place where you know that His will is good, pleasing, and perfect (Romans 12:2)? As Paul said:

"For me to live is Christ and to die is gain." (Philippians 1:21)

You can replace "cancer" with any of life's struggles, but the answer remains the same:

We either trust Him to see us through, knowing that "He who began a good work in you will carry it through to the end" (Philippians 1:6), or we don't, and by walking away, we show that we never had the saving faith that Jesus gives to any who truly believe.

On one occasion a rich young ruler came to Jesus wanting to know what he had to do to receive eternal life. (Mark 10:17-23) Jesus told him to go sell all that he had, give the money to the poor, and then come follow Him.

So why did Jesus demand that?

If he sold everything and gave it to the poor, he, his wife, and his family would end up in the poorhouse too and would need to beg to stay alive.

Is this what Jesus calls people to do to be His followers?

No, that's not the point. When you read the account in Mark, you will see that Jesus only mentions the last five commandments, bypassing the first of the commandments that deal with our relationship to God. Jesus was making the statement: These are the commandments you have failed to keep.

The first four commandments ask the question: Do you love God with all your heart, your soul, your mind, and your strength?

Jesus knew that this young man's god was his riches, and Mark concludes by saying, *"he went away sad"* because he was not willing to let money take second place in his life.

The apostle Paul reminded Timothy that *"the love of money is the root of all evil."* (1 Timothy 6:10).

For some, it is the amount of money in their bank accounts, the assets they own, or the value of their share portfolio that thrills them. For others, it is just the chase and challenge of making money and the gambles they take to gain wealth that excites them.

Either way, money can become a means of taking a person away from nurturing their relationship with God. How relevant is the question that Jesus asked:

"What will it profit a man if he gains the whole world and loses his soul? Or after he dies, what would he now give to buy back the opportunities lost?" (Mark 8:36-37).

Then there is pleasure. Someone once said that "the greatest pleasure in life is doing what people say you are not allowed to do." The pursuit of pleasure is seen as one of the highest priorities in Western culture—if not in the whole world.

This is the age of hedonism, a word that the Oxford Dictionary defines as "the pursuit of pleasure; sensual self-indulgence."

The Bible says that *"there is pleasure in sin for a season."* (Hebrews 11:25). But the pleasures of sin suffer from the law of diminishing returns.

What once gave pleasure no longer does after a short time, so the sensory organs of our body demand greater sensations to satisfy the hunger for pleasure. Whether it's drugs, sex, gambling, alcohol, or simply acquiring more possessions—the list is endless. There is an insatiable appetite for pleasure that is seldom satisfied in the hearts of mankind.

It was Pascal, the French philosopher, who gave the reason why we can't find fulfilment and satisfaction in life. He said we have a God-shaped hole in our lives that is so big only God can fill it.

The rock band U2 summed it up well in their song: "But still, I can't find what I'm looking for."

But the Bible says God will *"make known to me the path of life; He will fill me with joy in His presence, with eternal pleasures at His right hand."* (Psalm 16:11).

No wonder Jesus warned against allowing the weeds and the thorns of worries, riches, and pleasure to choke out the truth of the Gospel.

The Good Soil

Now we have the good soil—the people who received the message of the Gospel and received the person of Jesus, "the Seed." Because of His eternal life-giving power, His life began to reproduce itself within the lives of believers.

Matthew adds more insight in Matthew 13:8, stating that some people produced a crop—100 times, others 60 times, and others 30 times what was sown.

In other words, our Christian life is a growth process.

It's called sanctification—where we grow up into Christ, allowing His life to be expressed more fully within our lives. Paul spoke of this in Ephesians 5:8-21:

"For at one time you were darkness, but now you are light in the Lord. Walk as children of light (for the fruit of light is found in all that is good and right and true) and try to discern what is pleasing to the Lord.

Take no part in the unfruitful works of darkness, but instead expose them. For it is shameful even to speak of the things that they do in secret. But when anything is exposed by the light, it becomes visible, for anything that becomes visible is light. Therefore, it says, 'Awake, O sleeper, and arise from the dead, and Christ will shine on you.' Look carefully then how you walk, not as unwise but as wise, making the best use of the time, because the days are evil. Therefore, do not be foolish, but understand what the will of the Lord is. And do not get drunk with alcohol, for that is debauchery, but be filled with the Holy Spirit, addressing one another in psalms and hymns and spiritual songs, singing and making melody to the Lord with your heart, giving thanks always and for everything to God the Father in the name of our Lord Jesus Christ, submitting to one another out of reverence for Christ."

That's what a hundred-fold life would look like.

Final Reflection

"In Him is life, and His life was the light to mankind".

- Has God shone that light into your life yet?
- Do you recognise who Jesus is?
- Have you believed in Him and what He both teaches and has done for you on the cross?
- Have you embraced Him by faith and been born into His family as a child of God?
- Are you now taking those first steps to display that you are a follower of Him?

Our prayer for you is that you will see His light shine into your life and be saved.

Question Time: for chapter 7

Understanding the Parable of the Sower

1. The Hard Path – Jesus described some people as having hearts like a hard path where the seed cannot take root. What are some of the ways in which distractions, worldly reasoning, or personal pride can prevent people from accepting the Gospel? Have you ever experienced this in your own life?
2. The Rocky Ground – Jesus spoke of those who receive the Gospel with joy but fall away when testing comes. What are some challenges that might cause people to abandon their faith? How can we ensure that our faith is deeply rooted in Christ?
3. The Thorny Soil – Jesus identified worries, riches, and pleasures as things that can choke out faith. Which of these do you think is the greatest challenge for believers today? How can we guard against letting these things take priority over our relationship with God?

Personal Reflection and Application

1. Money and Faith – Jesus told the rich young ruler to sell all he had and follow Him. Why do you think Jesus asked this specific thing of him? What would be the equivalent challenge for people today?
2. Trusting God Through Trials – In Mark 8:36-37, Jesus asked, "What will it profit a man if he gains the whole world and loses his soul?" What does this verse mean to you personally? Have you ever struggled with trusting God's plan when things didn't go the way you expected?
3. Pleasure and Satisfaction – The study mentioned Pascal's idea of a "God-shaped hole" in our hearts. In what ways do people try to fill this void with things other than God? What does Psalm 16:11 teach us about where true joy is found?

Al Watson

Spiritual Growth and Living in the Light

1. Bearing Fruit in Different Measures – Matthew 13:8 speaks of believers producing fruit at different levels (100, 60, or 30 times what was sown). What do you think it means to bear fruit as a Christian? How can we cultivate a life that reflects a growing faith?
2. Being Rooted in Christ – Paul prayed for believers to be "rooted and established in love" (Ephesians 3:14-21). What are some practical ways we can deepen our relationship with God and strengthen our spiritual roots?
3. Shining the Light of Christ – Ephesians 5:8-21 encourages us to "walk as children of light." What does it look like to walk in the light in our daily lives? How can we be a light to others in a world filled with darkness?

Commitment and Response

1. A Personal Response to Jesus – The study ended with a challenge: Has God shone His light into your life? How would you describe your own faith journey right now? What steps can you take to grow closer to Jesus and live more fully as His follower?

Identity

Al Watson

Chapter Eight: Jesus the Lamb of God

Have you ever watched the sun rise in the morning? It starts with a dim glow but quickly progresses from the dimness of dawn to the brightness of noon.

That's a good illustration of how the Bible introduces us to Jesus, the Lamb of God. This is the sixth name for the Son of God in John chapter 1.

As you read the Bible, you will see how God's divine light progressively shines through all its pages, introducing us to "Jesus, the Lamb of God, who takes away the sins of the world."

There are many notable passages in which the lamb is progressively revealed.

In Genesis 22, we find the incident where Abraham offers a lamb in place of Isaac. This was at the same place Jesus was crucified.

In Exodus 12, there is the Passover Lamb, slain on the night before the Israelites escaped from Egypt. The Lamb protected them from judgement.

In Leviticus, there is the "lamb that is a sin offering," which the Israelites offered on the altar of sacrifice outside the tabernacle. This lamb died as their substitute.

In Isaiah 53, we see the suffering Saviour, led as a lamb to the slaughter, upon whom God laid the iniquity of us all.

In John 1:29, John the Baptist introduces us to Jesus: "Behold, the Lamb of God, who takes away the sins of the world."

In Acts 8, we read about the Ethiopian official returning home from Jerusalem in his chariot with his entourage on the Gaza Road. He was reading about the lamb in Isaiah 53. Philip the Evangelist explains that the lamb is Jesus the Messiah: *"Then Philip opened his mouth, and beginning with this Scripture, he told him the good news about Jesus"* (Acts 8:35).

1 Peter 1:18–21 tells us that we were redeemed with the precious blood of Christ, as of a lamb without blemish and without spot.

By calling Jesus a lamb, John the Baptiser was placing a death sentence on Him, because every lamb in the Bible was a slain lamb—a sacrificial lamb.

Speaking of His own death before the cross, Jesus told His disciples what would take place: *"He was teaching His disciples, saying to them, 'The Son of Man is going to be delivered into the hands of men, and they will kill Him. And when He is killed, after three days He will rise.' But they did not understand the saying and were afraid to ask Him"* (Mark 9:31).

The sacrificial death of Christ on the cross was the very reason Jesus came to earth.

The apostle Paul, throughout his letters to Christians, spoke of the cross of Jesus Christ as the most important point in his message. The Gospel—which is what he called the message he preached (Gospel means "good news")—is defined in 1 Corinthians 15:1–4:

"The gospel I preached to you, which you received, in which you stand, and by which you are being saved, if you hold fast to the word I preached to you—unless you believed in vain. For I delivered to you as of first importance what I also received: that Christ died for our sins in accordance with the Scriptures, that He was buried, that He was raised on the third day in accordance with the Scriptures…"

There are two names for Jesus that focus on the theme of the cross and how His death deals with the sin barrier that separated God and man. The first is Lamb of God; the second is Jesus, the eighth name given to God the Son: *"You shall call His name Jesus, for He shall save His people from their sin.*" (Matthew 1:21) Both names reveal how Jesus, through His sacrifice on the cross, deals with our sin. Jesus is the Lamb of God who came to take away the sin of the world.

When events occur that affect our lives and we know nothing about them until it's too late, it can be devastating. Cancer illustrates this well. A person may live their life totally unaware that they are suffering from colon cancer. Or for a woman, it may be breast cancer. These are very real conditions with life-and-death consequences, yet they may go unnoticed.

What happens in the physical world has a parallel in the spiritual world.

Your body is like a tent; it is only a temporary dwelling place. Because we are made in God's image, we are eternal beings. Though your body may be placed in the grave, your soul—your spirit—lives forever. The God who created us knows us completely.

He knows our thoughts. He knows our actions. He also knows the times we should have done good but did nothing.

The Bible calls such failures sin, for it says, "*He that knows to do good and fails to do it has sinned.*" (James 4:17)

We describe sins as either sins of commission—the things we do that are wrong—or sins of omission—the times we fail to do the good we should.

The Bible teaches that God has a record of every single sin we have ever committed. Yet most of us never contemplate a thought like that.

One day, however, we will stand before a holy God and answer for every wrong we have committed. This is why we needed Jesus to come as the Lamb of God—to take away the sins of the world. There are three stories in the Bible that illustrate what we need to know when thinking about Jesus as "The Lamb of God."

Through these historical accounts, we see how Jesus, as the Lamb of God, has dealt with sin and made it possible for God to forgive us.

The First Story: Abraham and Isaac

The first story is when Abraham was told to take his son Isaac and sacrifice him on Mount Moriah. We can read the record in Genesis 22. Isaac knew he was going with his father to worship God. He carried the wood for the offering, while his father had the knife and the fire. But Isaac wondered where the animal for the sacrifice was.

This is where the Bible is fascinating. Abraham answered his son, *"God will provide Himself a sacrifice."*

Did he really know what he was saying? The way he answered means that God would be the sacrifice. Little did he know that this is exactly what God would do in Jesus, for Jesus is Immanuel, God with us, and He is the Lamb of God who would die for the sins of the world.

When they arrived, they built the altar, laid the wood on it, and Abraham placed Isaac on the altar. Isaac was not a small child at this time; he could have resisted, but he willingly submitted, knowing that he would be resurrected because all the promises God had give his father where dependant on him being alive. At the last moment, God stopped Abraham and provided a ram as a substitute for Isaac. This powerful story illustrates four key lessons about the Lamb of God:

1. The location – Mount Moriah is the very place where Jerusalem was later built (2 Chronicles 3:1), and where Jesus was crucified as the Lamb of God outside the city walls.
2. Isaac's willingness – This reflects Jesus' willingness to lay down His life (John 10:17-18).
3. The substitute – The ram symbolises Christ, our substitutionary sacrifice. *"Christ died for our sins" 1 Corinthians 15:3*
4. Resurrection imagery – Isaac returned alive, foreshadowing Jesus 'resurrection after three days.

This story vividly illustrates the meaning behind the name Lamb of God, demonstrating how Jesus' sacrifice was planned by God for our redemption.

The Second Story: The Scapegoat

The second story is the story of the scapegoat in Leviticus 16. This took place on the most solemn day for the nation of Israel—Yom Kippur, or the Day of Atonement. One of the sacrificial acts that took place on that day involved two goats. One goat was sacrificed, and its blood was sprinkled on the altar of the temple. This illustrated that a substitutionary death had taken place, as this goat died instead of all the people in the land of Israel.

The second goat was called the scapegoat. Aaron the priest was told to:

"Place his hands on the head of the live goat and confess over it all the iniquities of the people of Israel, and all their transgressions, all their sins. And he shall put them on the head of the goat and send it away into the wilderness by the hand of a man in readiness." (Leviticus 16:21) In this illustration, God shows us what He does with sin once we receive forgiveness by placing our trust and faith in Jesus' death. We ask Jesus to be our substitute. Remember what John the Baptist said: *"Behold, the Lamb of God who takes away"*—that means He removes— *"the sins of the world."*

The first goat symbolically bore the sins of the nation of Israel. However, when the second goat was taken into the wilderness and left there, God illustrated that He removes sin from His people.

"For as high as the heavens are above the earth, so great is His steadfast love toward those who fear Him; as far as the east is from the west, so far does He remove our transgressions from us." (Psalm 103:11-12) There is no point where east and west meet.

"He will again have compassion on us; He will tread our iniquities underfoot. You will cast all our sins into the depths of the sea." (Micah 7:19)

This story powerfully illustrates how Jesus, as the Lamb of God, not only bears our sins but removes them completely.

The Third Story: The Ethiopian Official

The third story is found in Acts 8, where Philip, a preacher, was instructed by God to leave a city in Samaria and go to a desert road leading from Jerusalem to Gaza. This seemed unusual, as there were no people living there. However, Philip obeyed.

On the road, he encountered a caravan from Ethiopia. The treasurer of Ethiopia, seated in a chariot, was reading from the Prophet Isaiah. He had travelled to Jerusalem seeking the one true God and had acquired the writings of Isaiah. Philip was directed by God to approach the chariot.

Philip asked, *"Do you understand what you are reading?"* The Ethiopian replied, *"How can I, unless someone guides me?"* He was reading Isaiah 53: *"Like a sheep he was led to the slaughter, and like a lamb before its shearer is silent, so he opens not his mouth..."*

The Ethiopian asked Philip to join him in the chariot and asked, who this was referring to. Philip then shared the good news of Jesus, the Lamb of God. Recognising Jesus as God's substitute for his sin, the Ethiopian believed, embracing Jesus as his God and saviour. Upon passing a body of water, he asked to be baptised.

Philip baptised him, symbolising his unity with Jesus in death, burial, and resurrection (Colossians 2:12-15).

This story demonstrates that Jesus, the Lamb of God, calls us to believe, be baptised, and live the resurrected life in Him.

Conclusion

Jesus, the Lamb of God, died in our place as our substitute, making it possible for God to forgive us and remove our sins eternally. As Charles Spurgeon once said:

"When God looks at you, He sees Jesus, because when God looked at Jesus on the cross, He saw you." Now that you have learned more about Jesus, share this knowledge with others, for the best way to learn is to teach.

Question Time: For chapter 8

1. Progressive Revelation of the Lamb
   - How does the concept of Jesus as the Lamb of God develop throughout the Bible, from Genesis to Revelation?
   - What does this progressive revelation teach us about God's plan for redemption?

2. The Substitutionary Sacrifice
   - In Genesis 22, Abraham says, "God will provide Himself a sacrifice." How does this foreshadow Jesus 'role as the Lamb of God?
   - What does Isaac's willingness to be sacrificed teach us about Jesus 'attitude towards His own crucifixion? Support your answers with scripture.

3. The Passover and Jesus
   - How does the Passover lamb in Exodus 12 parallel Jesus 'sacrifice on the cross?
   - What does this reveal about the significance of Jesus 'blood in our salvation?

4. The Scapegoat and the Removal of Sin
   - What is the significance of the two goats in Leviticus 16?
   - How does this help us understand Jesus 'role not only in bearing sin but also in removing it from us?

5. Isaiah 53 and the Suffering Servant
   - How does Isaiah 53 describe the suffering of the Lamb of God?
   - Why was it important for Jesus to suffer in order to bring salvation?

6. John the Baptist's Proclamation
   - When John the Baptist declares, "Behold, the Lamb of God, who takes away the sin of the world," what does this statement reveal about Jesus 'mission?
   - How would this statement have been understood by John's audience?

7. Philip and the Ethiopian Official
   - How does Philip's encounter with the Ethiopian official in Acts 8 demonstrate the power of Scripture in revealing Jesus as the Lamb of God?
   - What role does personal evangelism play in leading others to Christ?

8. The Cross as the Central Message
   - Why does Paul emphasise the cross as the most important part of the gospel message in 1 Corinthians 15?
   - How does the cross deal with the sin barrier between God and humanity?

9. The Reality of Sin and the Need for a Saviour
   - This chapter compares physical ailments like cancer to sin. How does this analogy help us understand the seriousness of sin?
   - Why do people often ignore their spiritual condition, and how can we help them see their need for salvation.

10. Responding to Jesus, the Lamb of God

- What does it mean personally to accept Jesus as the Lamb of God?
- How can we live out this truth in our daily lives and share it with others?

Identity

Al Watson

Chapter Nine: His Name is Jesus

In this chapter, we are looking at the seventh name for Jesus in John chapter one, which is the name we are all familiar with: Jesus. Our goal is to understand the person, purpose, and character of Jesus because this is who we are asked to commit our eternal destiny to.

We talk about the five steps involved in coming to a faith commitment based on John 1:10-13, where we:

1. Recognise who Jesus is.
2. Believe in Him.
3. Receive Him or embrace Him as our God and Saviour.
4. Become a child of God after being born again into His family. From here on, we start
5. Following Jesus. He is the teacher, and we are the students. So, let's get into today's chapter, where we are looking at the name "Jesus."

The best-known name for God the Son is Jesus. This was the name given to Him when the angel, who was sent by God to Mary, told her she was going to be the mother of the promised Saviour. The angel said, "You shall call His name Jesus" (Luke 1:31).

The word or name Jesus is the Greek form of the Hebrew name Joshua, which means "The Lord is Salvation" or "The Salvation of the Lord."

Joseph was engaged to Mary, but during their engagement, Joseph discovered that Mary was pregnant. Knowing he was not the father of that child, he wanted to break their engagement, but God sent an angel to inform Joseph of what was happening.

Matthew gives us the interaction between the angel and Joseph in Matthew 1:18–21:

"Now the birth of Jesus Christ took place in this way. When His mother Mary had been engaged to Joseph, before they came together, she was found to be with child from the Holy Spirit. And her husband Joseph, being a just man and unwilling to put her to shame, resolved to divorce her quietly. But as he considered these things, behold, an angel of the Lord appeared to him in a dream, saying, 'Joseph, son of David, do not fear to take Mary as your wife, for that which is conceived in her is from the Holy Spirit. She will bear a son, and you shall call His name Jesus, for He will save His people from their sins.'"

When we talk about Jesus saving us from our sins, we ask the question, "How did He do this?" I believe that we answered that when we studied His name, Lamb of God. We looked at His death, burial, and resurrection, where Jesus is seen as the substitutionary offering in our place. We recognise the benefits or blessings that we receive from His salvation. As Paul says in 1 Corinthians 6:11, we have "been washed, we have been sanctified, we are justified in the Name of the Lord Jesus Christ and by the Spirit of our God."

However, there is another question that we need to ask: "What did Jesus save us from?"

Let me illustrate what we mean. If you were swimming in the ocean and suddenly a strong rip dragged you under the water, hopefully, you would raise your hand, hoping that a lifeguard would see it. When the lifeguard swims out to you, he will rescue you from drowning. This makes him your saviour.

So, what did he save you from? From death by drowning.

We need to be clear about what Jesus has saved us for and from. In this chapter, I want us to look at that question and consider what Jesus saves us from.

John 3:36 is a good place to start in answering this question:

John 3:35-36: "The Father loves the Son and has given all things into His hand. Whoever believes in the Son has eternal life; whoever does not obey the Son shall not see life, but the wrath of God remains on him."

The Apostle Paul says the same in 1 Thessalonians 1:9-10: "… you turned to God from idols to serve the living and true God, and to wait for His Son from heaven, whom He raised from the dead, Jesus who delivers us from the wrath to come."

As a pastor of a church, you sometimes face heartbreaking moments. One I remember was when I sat with a young wife beside her dying husband. The husband was on a life support machine, but he was brain dead.

Hepatitis had killed him. The wife was six months pregnant, and now her husband would never see his son or experience all the joys and promise that their future could have held. We both watched the doctor turn the life support machine off.

Moments like that are real, and they carry truths that we never want to face. The same is true with this question: "What does Jesus save us from?" Facing the implications of a topic like this is unsettling. But to ignore it is unwise. You might hate a doctor telling you that you have cancer, but it is only when you face the reality of your health that you will seek treatment.

If we know the God of the Bible and His Son, Jesus Christ, with a personal relationship, then, as John says in chapter 17:3, we have eternal life:

"And this is eternal life, that they know you, the only true God, and Jesus Christ whom you have sent."

Knowing God and Jesus with this personal relationship gives us eternal life. Or, as John explained it in 1 John 5:11–12:

"And this is the testimony, that God gave us eternal life, and this life is in His Son. Whoever has the Son has life; whoever does not have the Son of God does not have life."

Eternal life comes when we are united with Jesus, by faith, in His death, burial, and resurrection. You may ask, how can that happen?

Although the crucifixion of Jesus took place over 2,000 years ago, God, in His thinking, placed all who were to believe in Jesus into the death of Jesus so that His death paid the debt of our sin, even though we were not yet born. "Even as He chose us in Him before the foundation of the world, that we should be holy and blameless before Him" (Ephesians 1:4). As the Bible says, "Christ died for our sins, according to the

Scriptures" (1 Corinthians 15:3).

Then the Holy Spirit brings all the benefits of the risen Lord Jesus Christ into our lives; our eternal destiny is now very different from those Paul described in Ephesians 2:12, where he says that people without Jesus are people without God and without hope.

Or, to use Paul's words in Romans 8:1: *"There is therefore now no condemnation for those who are in Christ Jesus."*

Again, I ask the question, "What are we saved from?" John 3:36: "The wrath of God."

God is both the Creator of all that is and, therefore, the Owner of all that is. Psalm 24:1: *"The earth is the Lord's and the fullness thereof, the world and those who dwell therein."*

Al Watson

We know that God *"so loved the world…"* (John 3:16), and we are told that *"God is love"* (1 John 4:8). It is in His character to act in love. So where does this wrath and judgment fit into a God of love?

When we explore God's character, it's important to distinguish between His attributes and His actions. Judgment and wrath are not core aspects of who God is; rather, they are necessary responses that arise from His nature. A just God must confront injustice, and a holy God cannot overlook unholiness.

God's judgments are never arbitrary. Even in His justice, He remains faithful, merciful, gracious, and loving—His character never changes.

In perfect consistency, God provides justice for all who turn to Him. He does exactly what He has promised while extending mercy to those who do not deserve it. The book of Revelation vividly depicts God's wrath toward sinful humanity, but it also reveals humanity's response: *"The rest of mankind… did not repent and did not stop worshipping demons."* (Revelation 9:20).

Throughout Revelation, the last book in the Bible, we see that God continuously gives people the opportunity to repent and turn to Him. His judgment is not about destruction but about restoring people to Himself. His goal is not vengeance; it is compassion. God does not exercise His power and justice purely to punish—rather, He does so as an invitation to return to Him.

In every act of judgment, God is calling: "Come back to me." His perfect character remains steadfast.

Even if we accept that God is perfect, we may struggle with the severity of His judgments. Why does a loving God bring judgment? At first glance, it might seem that love and judgment are incompatible. But when we consider the evil in this world, we recognise that justice is necessary. No one truly wants a God who turns a blind eye to wrongdoing.

Identity

When we witness injustice, we long for fairness. We desire a God who is both gracious and just—someone who holds wrongdoers accountable while offering grace to those who seek it. We want justice infused with love and love that upholds justice.

This raises a common question: What about good, kind-hearted people who don't profess faith in Jesus?

Many dedicate their lives to helping others, supporting the disadvantaged, and giving generously—how can they be judged the same way as those who commit unspeakable crimes?

Ultimately, judgment is not just about our actions; it is about whether we accept or reject God. Paul explains this in Romans 1:18-32, where he describes how humanity suppresses the truth of God's existence despite being His creation. God intended for us to experience life in its fullest, yet many choose to ignore or deny Him.

Because of this rebellion, judgment is inevitable. Jesus first came to bring salvation, but He will return as the judge of all people. John 5:22: *"For the Father judges no one, but has given all judgment to the Son."*

If we continually tell ourselves something false, we may eventually come to believe it as truth. However, repetition does not change reality. Many people spend their lives embracing a falsehood, believing that ignoring or rejecting the truth will somehow make it disappear.

Psalm 24:1 declares: *"The earth belongs to God! Everything in all the world is His!"*

One day, every person will stand before God and be held accountable for the life they were given. Some assume that judgment is based solely on actions—that living a good life is enough to avoid condemnation.

However, Scripture makes it clear that judgment is centred on one pivotal question: "What have you done with Jesus?"

John 3:36 states: *"Whoever believes in the Son has eternal life; whoever does not obey the Son shall not see life, but the wrath of God remains on him."*

If someone rejects Jesus, they are held accountable for every sin they have ever committed. God is holy, just, and true, and as Colossians 3:25 affirms: *"For the wrongdoer will be paid back for the wrong he has done, and there is no partiality."* The greatest wrong is our rejection.

2 Thessalonians 1:8-9 sheds light on the judgement and why: *"Inflicting vengeance on those who do not know God and on those who do not obey the gospel of our Lord Jesus. They will suffer the punishment of eternal destruction, away from the presence of the Lord and from the glory of His might."*

Imagine cutting flowers from a garden. Though they may appear alive for a while in water, they have already been severed from their source of life and will continue to decay until we through them out. Similarly, rejecting God—the true source of life—leads to death.

Before their rebellion, Adam and Eve lived with an unending life, because they were connected to God.

But when they chose their own way, they lost that relationship. As a result, humanity entered a state of spiritual death, as well as physical death and all the physical consequences of the degenerating impact of sin. We carry their DNA in our bodies as we read in Romans 5:12 *"Therefore, just as sin came into the world through one man, and death through sin, and so death spread to all men because all sinned."*

We are God's creation, yet why do we ignore, reject, or even oppose Him? Some display this rebellion passively, through indifference; others are more openly resistant.

Physical death happens when the body ceases to function. But beyond physical death, there is a second, eternal death—one where God, as judge, allows people to spend eternity separated from Him, based on their own choice, because they choose not to repent.

In the final book of the Bible, Revelation, the Apostle John records a vision from God that describes the ultimate fate of those who reject the salvation offered through Jesus.

The Reality of Judgment

Revelation 20:11-15 paints a sobering picture of the final judgment:

"Then I saw a great white throne, and Him who was seated on it. From His presence, earth and sky fled away, and no place was found for them. And I saw the dead, great and small, standing before the throne, and books were opened. Then another book was opened, which is the book of life. And the dead were judged by what was written in the books, according to what they had done. And the sea gave up the dead who were in it; Death and Hades gave up the dead who were in them, and they were judged, each one of them, according to what they had done. Then Death and Hades were thrown into the lake of fire. This is the second death—the lake of fire. And if anyone's name was not found written in the book of life, he was thrown into the lake of fire."

This is a reality many prefer to ignore, but turning a blind eye to it does not change its certainty. I have no intention of being alarmist or manipulating emotions through fear. My only aim is to remain faithful to God's Word. If we do not grasp the seriousness of our situation, we will see no reason to change.

The Nature of Separation from God

How can we describe the horror of being eternally separated from God and, at the same time, the beauty of the life He offers?

The Bible provides five vivid illustrations to help us understand what it means to be cut off from Jesus. Jesus frequently used real-world imagery to convey deep spiritual truths. Whether these descriptions are literal or symbolic is irrelevant—the reality they represent is beyond human comprehension.

Fire—A Lake of Fire

For those of us living in Australia, particularly along the eastern seaboard, the devastation caused by fire is all too familiar. Australia is one of the most fire-prone regions in the world. In 2020, we experienced the most catastrophic bushfires in our nation's history. The destruction was immense 2,779 homes lost, 34 lives taken, and 186,000 square kilometres of land consumed. Entire landscapes were reduced to smouldering embers.

Jesus describes hell as a lake of fire. Whether this fire is literal or figurative, the reality it conveys is excruciating suffering. If fire is being used as a metaphor, it still represents something of unbearable torment. Just as those who lost everything in the bushfires stood before the charred remains of their homes, those in hell will endure the eternal realisation of everything they have lost.

Worm That Does Not Die

Jesus also speaks of judgment using another unsettling image—the worm that never dies.

Mark 9:48 describes hell as a place where *"the worm does not die, and the fire is not quenched."*

Where there is death, there is decay, and worms consume what is left. As a farmer, I have witnessed this many times when an animal has died maggots take over the decomposing body.

Jesus uses this image to illustrate the internal torment of those who are eternally separated from Him. This unending anguish is burdened with guilt, shame, and regret—memories that gnaw at the soul like a worm that never ceases to feed. Death is not the end; it is the beginning of eternity.

In this eternal judgment, the weight of losing everything once known and loved, combined with the haunting realisation that it could have been prevented, becomes the very essence of torment. The relentless regret and inescapable awareness of what was lost—that is what makes the gnawing memory of hell unbearable.

Outer Darkness

Matthew 22:13 provides another powerful image of judgment. In this passage, Jesus tells a parable about a king who hosts a wedding feast for his son. All who attended were given new garments, which symbolise the righteousness provided by God through faith in Christ. However, one man refused to wear the wedding clothes, representing those who reject God's offer of salvation.

In response, the king commands his servants:

"Bind him hand and foot and cast him into the outer darkness. In that place, there will be weeping and gnashing of teeth."

Jesus describes hell as a place of absolute darkness—separation from the presence of God, the source of all goodness, joy, and light.

Weeping

John 3:19-20 explains why people reject salvation:

"This is the judgment: The light has come into the world, and people loved darkness rather than light because their works were evil. For everyone who does wicked things hates the light and does not come to the light, lest his works should be exposed."

Many prefer to remain in darkness, choosing their own way rather than God's truth. In the end, God grants them what they desire—eternal existence apart from Him. But in that darkness, there will be endless sorrow.

Those who rejected Christ will come to the dreadful realisation of their decision, and weeping will be their response.

Al Watson

Gnashing of Teeth

Alongside weeping, Jesus describes gnashing of teeth—an expression of fear, deep regret, frustration, and despair. Those who rejected salvation will recall every opportunity they had to accept God's forgiveness, but by then, it will be too late.

Romans 8:1 offers the hope they could have embraced: *"There is therefore now no condemnation for those who are in Christ Jesus."*

The Question of Forgiveness

How can God forgive sinners? God does not overlook sin. Like a ledger filled with debts, every wrong must be accounted for. Justice demands that the books be balanced. This is where Jesus comes in—He took upon Himself the judgment we deserved. God can forgive because Christ bore our punishment on the cross. As an old hymn beautifully puts it:

"He who knew them laid them on Him, and now believing, we are free."

Jesus came with one purpose: "They shall call His name Jesus, for He will save His people from their sins."

A Lesson from the Pandemic

The COVID-19 pandemic reminded us how quickly life can change. My home state of Victoria was hit the hardest in Australia, leading to a state of emergency. Strict lockdowns were enforced residents could leave their homes for only one hour a day, only one household member could shop for essentials, and movement was restricted within a 5km radius. A curfew from 8 PM to 5 AM was imposed, and violations resulted in hefty fines.

One night, 77 individuals deliberately broke the curfew, believing the rules to be unfair. Each of them was fined $1,652. Regardless of their personal opinions, the law was clear, and they had to face the consequences of their choices.

The same principle applies to rejecting Jesus Christ. John 3:16-20 makes it plain: "*For God so loved the world, that He gave His only Son, that whoever believes in Him should not perish but have eternal life... Whoever believes in Him is not condemned, but whoever does not believe is condemned already.*" God does not force anyone into judgment—people choose their own destiny.

The Final Choice

In the end, God simply gives people what they desire. Those who long to be with Him will enjoy eternal fellowship in His presence. Those who reject Him will be eternally separated from Him in a place too terrible to fully describe.

Before his death, Joshua, the great leader of Israel, challenged the people with these words: "*Put away the gods your ancestors served... Choose this day whom you will serve... But as for me and my house, we will serve the Lord.*"

This challenge remains relevant today. What will your choice be?

Al Watson

Here are 10 questions based on our notes: Chapter 9.

1. What does the name "Jesus" personally mean to you, and how has your understanding of it deepened through this study?

2. In what ways have you experienced the five steps of faith commitment (recognition, belief, receiving, becoming, and following Jesus) in your own life?

3. Jesus came to save us from sin and its consequences. How has this truth shaped your perspective on salvation and God's grace?

4. Reflect on a time when you struggled with doubt or obedience in your faith. How does knowing Jesus as your Saviour help you navigate such moments?

5. What does the concept of God's wrath and judgment mean to you? How does it influence the way you share your faith with others?

6. The study mentions different images of separation from God (fire, darkness, weeping, etc.). Which of these resonates with you the most, and why?

7. How does the reality of judgment challenge the way you live your daily life and make decisions?

8. Many people struggle with the idea that "good people" also need salvation. How would you explain the necessity of faith in Jesus to someone who believes in being "good" as enough?

9. How does understanding Jesus as both Saviour and Judge impact your relationship with Him?

10. If you had to summarise the key takeaway from this study in one sentence, what would it be, and how will you apply it in your life?

Identity

Al Watson

Chapter Ten: Jesus The Teacher

We now come to the eighth description of Jesus. He is called "Rabbi," a Hebrew word that means "my master, my teacher." John 1:38

On one occasion, the religious leaders sent the temple guards to arrest Jesus. However, as they listened to his teaching, they returned without arresting him. When challenged as to why they failed to bring him before the court, they simply said, *"No one ever spoke like this man."* (John 7:46)

The Gospel of Mark records the time when Jesus went to the synagogue on the Sabbath (Mark 1:21–28):

"And they went into Capernaum, and immediately on the Sabbath he entered the synagogue and was teaching. And they were astonished at his teaching, for he taught them as one who had authority, and not as the scribes. And immediately there was in their synagogue a man with an unclean spirit. And he cried out, 'What have you to do with us, Jesus of Nazareth? Have you come to destroy us? I know who you are—the Holy One of God.' But Jesus rebuked him, saying, 'Be silent, and come out of him!' And the unclean spirit, convulsing him and crying out with a loud voice, came out of him. And they were all amazed, so that they questioned among themselves, saying, 'What is this? A new teaching with authority! He commands even the unclean spirits, and they obey him.' And at once his fame spread everywhere throughout all the surrounding region of Galilee."

The Authority of Jesus' Teaching

As you read the Gospels, you will be struck by the impact of Jesus' message on his audience. But what stands out is not his oratory skill or the range of his vocabulary, but rather the simplicity of his style and the demands his message places on the lives of his listeners. Mark rightly concluded that people *"were astonished at his teaching, for he taught them as one who had authority."*

Jesus was no ordinary teacher; he was the promised Messiah sent by God. The prophet Isaiah, some 800 years before the birth of Jesus, informed us that Jesus would be a great teacher and the source of great wisdom:

Isaiah 11:2

"And the Spirit of the Lord shall rest upon him, the Spirit of wisdom and understanding, the Spirit of counsel and might, the Spirit of knowledge and the fear of the Lord."

Such wisdom should not surprise us, because Jesus is "The Truth" (John 14:6). Wisdom, understanding, counsel, and knowledge underpinned all that he taught.

The Clash Between Jesus and the Intellectuals

Jesus often clashed with the intellectuals of his day who ignored the plain teaching from their Old Testament book, Proverbs. In chapter 3:5, there is a line drawn between two kinds of wisdom in the world:

"Trust in the Lord with all your heart, and do not lean on your own understanding." There is God's wisdom and then there is the wisdom of man.

Similarly, the Apostle Paul highlighted that the value system underpinning worldly thinking will never enable a person to understand God's wisdom:

1. Corinthians 2:14

"The natural person does not accept the things of the Spirit of God, for they are folly to him, and he is not able to understand them because they are spiritually discerned."

Seeking God's Wisdom

Returning to the book of Proverbs, we find that accessing God's wisdom requires making a choice. Then there is the New Testament, which makes it clear that discovering the truth demands a willingness to think things through.

2. Timothy 2:7 "*Think over what I say, for the Lord will give you understanding in everything.*"

King Solomon sought to teach his son about God's wisdom, emphasising the responsibility to seek and act upon the truth. Notice how he repeatedly says "if you," implying a conscious choice:

"*My son, if you receive my words and treasure up my commandments with you, making your ear attentive to wisdom and inclining your heart to understanding; yes, if you call out for insight and raise your voice for understanding, if you seek it like silver and search for it as for hidden treasures, then you will understand the fear (reverence) of the Lord and find the knowledge of God.*" Proverbs 2:1-5

God has truth that we need to know, and He will teach us if we truly seek it. However, we live in a world dominated by relativism, where people believe that their version of truth is just as valid as anyone else's. This has led many to dismiss the idea of absolute truth altogether.

Yet, this is just another attempt to do away with God's truth. That truth is personified in Jesus, for He is "*the Way, the Truth, and the Life*" (John 14:6).

Understanding the Message of Jesus

The message of Jesus is just information unless it is believed and accepted. Simply listening to his teaching and wisdom makes little difference unless one acts upon it. There were lots of people who listened to Jesus and never really understood the wisdom of his message.

Do you want to know why? They didn't really want to know. It's a paradox but so true. Being able to understand and know the message of

Jesus has far more to do with our will than our mind. Jesus put it this way in John 7:17: *"If anyone is willing, he shall know the truth."*

Jesus didn't say that understanding was dependent on the degree of intelligence, our religious background, the country of our birth, or our gender. He said, *if you want to know, you can know,* because He will make it known to you.

"If anyone is willing, they shall know."

There is an old saying that explains why so many people don't engage with the teaching of Jesus Christ, the Son of God:

"Don't confuse me with facts; my mind is made up."

Or, as another saying puts it:

"There is no one so blind as those that don't want to see."

The Real Message of Jesus

Jesus came to seek and to save the lost. If you could reduce His message down to its irreducible minimum, it is always focused on achieving that. But the issue He faced was that people did not recognise that they were lost. Yet that is exactly what God says we are—lost.

The Son of God and the Real Message

The Son of God, who became a man to teach the world the only way of salvation, is basically ignored because people don't want to know. They might want what Jesus offers, but they don't want Him, and so they turn a blind eye to what He teaches.

It is interesting to know that if you're struggling to understand, you're not alone. His disciples spent 3+ years listening to Jesus teach, and they never really understood what His teaching meant. That was until Jesus did something for them. And what He did for the disciples, He will do for you—if you really want to know.

You read of the event in Luke 24:44–49:

Then he said to them, "These are my words that I spoke to you while I was still with you, that everything written about me in the Law of Moses and the Prophets and the Psalms must be fulfilled." Then he opened their minds to understand the Scriptures, and said to them, "Thus it is written, that the Christ should suffer and on the third day rise from the dead, and that repentance for the forgiveness of sins should be proclaimed in his name to all nations, beginning from Jerusalem. You are witnesses of these things. And behold, I am sending the promise of my Father upon you. But stay in the city until you are clothed with power from on high."

Did you catch what Jesus said?

"He opened their minds to understand the Scriptures." He opened their minds.

We know that the disciples wanted to know, for they faithfully followed Jesus for 3+ years. So that first part—*if anyone is willing, he shall know*—was clearly seen. But now, the next step required to understand the real meaning of the teaching of Jesus needed God to step in and do something.

You notice we have said "the real meaning."

Many people take the teaching of Jesus and limit it to a framework of moral principles that will help them make decisions in life.

They often take some of the principles in the Sermon on the Mount as an example and confess that these principles give them their moral guidelines for life:

- Don't get angry, because it could lead to murder.
- Don't look lustfully at a person of the opposite sex, because that could lead you to commit adultery.
- When you say *yes* to something, mean what you say.

- Don't point the finger at other people who have done something wrong and act as their judge and jury. Recognise the fact that you probably have just as many sins on your own record.
- Do to other people the kind of things you want them to do to you.

These are just five principles that are based on the teachings of Jesus, and they are basically saying *prevention is better than the cure.*

But Jesus teaches that for you to be able to live like this requires something supernatural to happen within your own life first.

And that is why we say we really need to focus on the real message of Jesus before we will ever be able to live life the way life should be lived.

So, What Is the Real Message of Jesus?

To find the answer to what was the real message—the number one priority in the message of Jesus—you only have to go back to His stated purpose for coming:

He came to seek and to save that which was lost.

He is the great teacher, and His message always revolved around the ways to bring the lostness and the way to receive God's salvation before people.

He came to seek and save the lost!

The problem that we have in our world is that we don't recognise we are lost. Yet that is exactly what God says we are—LOST.

If you look at three of His messages, you will get a clear understanding of what He means by saving the lost.

The first is in His first recorded message:

Mark 1:14

"Jesus came into Galilee, proclaiming the gospel of God, and saying, 'The time is fulfilled, and the kingdom of God is at hand; repent and believe in the gospel.'"

What did He mean by "repent"?

Repent means "to have a change of mind" or to turn around and start going in the opposite direction.

The change of mind that is needed is in relation to God.

Paul put it this way in Acts 20:20-21: *"How I did not shrink from declaring to you anything that was profitable, and teaching you in public and from house to house, testifying both to Jews and to Greeks <u>of repentance toward God and of faith in our Lord Jesus Christ.</u>"*

Repentance means we need to stop ignoring God and living a life opposed to all that God desires of us. The change in our thinking requires, as Hebrews 11:6 says, "And without faith it is impossible to please him, for whoever would draw near to God must believe that he exists and that he rewards those who seek him." Do you believe that God exists?

There is a misunderstanding about what is meant by repentance. Some give the impression that it is about changing your lifestyle—you stop doing destructive behaviours and you "get your act together," so to speak. Then, with that kind of change, you can find acceptance with God. That is entirely wrong. You will change your life, but it will be because you now don't want to participate in those behaviours.

People can change their behaviours with a lot of effort. For example, we have Alcoholics Anonymous to help you kick alcohol, and there are programs that help you with anger management, along with many other self-help programmes.

Repentance is about getting right in your attitude towards God and being willing to believe in Him and submit to Him in all aspects of your life. The desire to do that will grow out of being "born again," to use the words of John 3:3. Perhaps Philippians 2:13 explains it best: "For it is God who works in you, both to will and to work for his good pleasure."

The Next Step to Notice

The next step to notice can be seen in a conversation Jesus has with a key leader in Israel. His name was Nicodemus:

"Truly, truly, I say to you, unless one is born again he cannot see the kingdom of God."

"That which is born of the flesh is flesh, and that which is born of the Spirit is spirit. Do not marvel that I said to you, 'You must be born again.'"

So, this Kingdom of God is entered—which means we now bow to a different ruler, a King, a Leader, a Sovereign in our lives—and His name is Jesus. It was Jesus who made this possible through His death, burial, and resurrection. Now the Holy Spirit will bring this reality into your life by giving new life to that part of you which was dead and dormant from the day you were born: your spirit.

When this takes place, a person can start a new life:

2 Corinthians 5:17-18 *"Therefore, if anyone is in Christ, he is a new creation. The old has passed away; behold, the new has come. All this is from God, who through Christ reconciled us to himself."*

Jesus spent the rest of His ministry preaching this message to the spiritually lost people who crowded to hear Him.

As examples, take three parables that Jesus strung together in Luke 15.

Jesus was speaking to religious leaders who had just condemned Him for spending time teaching the tax collectors and sinners—people that these religious leaders would call the scum of the earth. They were not worthy of being spoken to let alone eating with them as Jesus did.

First of the three parables

Jesus starts with the first of the three parables. It was about a farmer who had 100 sheep. When he counts them into a new field, he finds that one is missing. The shepherd goes after the lost sheep, and when he finds it, he puts it on his shoulder and comes home, so thankful that he found what was lost.

Now the punchline of this story is that the religious leaders were responsible for caring for the people within their fold. They were supposed to be the shepherds within the community.

They were responsible for seeking out the lost and broken within their communities. But that would have been the farthest thing on their minds, for such people were beneath them.

However, as far as heaven was concerned, there would be more rejoicing in heaven over one soul that returned to God seeking His forgiveness and reconciliation than over 99 so called righteous people who thought they did not need to repent.

Unlike the religious leaders, Jesus was the Good Shepherd who came to seek and to save the lost.

Because *"all we like sheep have gone astray and turned everyone to his own ways"*—to quote Isaiah 53:6—we too need to be found by Jesus.

The Second Story

The second story was that of a woman who lost one of ten coins.

There is no record as to why these coins were important, but the point being made is in what this woman did in her determination to find her lost coin.

She gets a light, sweeps the house, and seeks diligently.

Think for a minute: with the lost sheep, a sheep could respond by bleating, which would give the shepherd some direction in finding it.

However, the lost coin could contribute nothing toward being found. It was up to the diligence of the seeker.

That was Jesus' point—we all have the responsibility to seek the lost. How far would you go toward seeking lost souls?

Here, Jesus shows how far He would go—by dining with these outcasts in order to seek to win them.

The Final Story

The final story was about two sons and their father.

One son was sick of home and wanted his inheritance so that he could go and live it up in a world that seemed to offer so much more than what he experienced at home.

Despite breaking his father's heart, the father gave him the money, and off he went.

It didn't take long for his wealth to be squandered, and soon he was left begging for food just to stay alive.

As he thought about his future, he realised it would be better to go home and see if his father would take him on as a servant—that way, at least he would have food to eat and a roof over his head.

But as he approached, he saw his father running towards him, and when they reached each other, his father threw his arms around his lost son, calling the servants to bring new clothes. Then his father put a ring on his finger and told the servants to kill the fattened calf and prepare a feast:

"For this son of mine was dead but now he is alive, he was lost but now he is home."

When the eldest son came in from the field and found that the celebration was for his brother who had returned, he was furious and ranted at his father for welcoming this prodigal home.

The point of the story is that these religious leaders were just like the older brother, who had no compassion for those who were lost—the very people Jesus sat and ate with: the publicans and sinners.

The religious leaders were totally unaware of the hardness of their hearts towards the people around them, and therefore, towards God. Yet, they believed they were God's servants on earth. How deluded they were!

Looking Into His Word

If we fail to investigate His Word—the Bible—and discover the reason we are lost, we will never find out what it is that controls our lives and why we need salvation.

It is in the Bible that Jesus puts His finger on what really motivates the way people live their lives. Look at what He says about the basic problem in our world today and where the motivations for our behaviours come from:

"But what comes out of the mouth proceeds from the heart, and this defiles a person. For out of the heart come evil thoughts, murder, adultery, sexual immorality, theft, false witness, slander. These are what defile a person." Matthew 15:18-20

Jesus, the teacher, is saying we have a heart problem—and He is not talking about the pump that circulates your blood.

He is talking about the real you—your inner being, your personality, your soul.

This is why we need saving.

Look at the list—which is far from complete—evil thoughts, murder, adultery, sexual immorality, theft, false witness, slander.

Also, remember that it's not just the action—the thought or contemplation of doing something wrong is where the action starts, generated by our lostness.

He came to seek and to save the lost.!

Our lostness is not only seen in our actions—it is also seen in our speech.

"For out of the abundance of the heart, the mouth speaks."

He goes on to say:

"I tell you, on the day of judgment people will give an account for every careless word they speak, for by your words you will be justified, and by your words you will be condemned."

This might be a revelation moment for us, for it reveals that what drives our actions and thoughts needs a dramatic change—the kind that Jesus can bring.

I wonder if you are wanting the salvation that Jesus came to bring.

If that is so, then look at what John says in chapter 1, verse 12:

"But to all (that includes you) who receive him, who believed in his name, he gave the right to become children of God, who were born, not of blood, nor the will of the flesh, nor the will of man, but of God."

So these verses tell us that we can have a new life given to us—we can have a second birth. This birth is something that God causes—He gives us a new life.

Three Things to Notice

I want you to notice the three things that take place here:

1. There is someone to receive into our lives—that is Jesus.
2. There is something to believe—that Jesus is the Son of God, that He died on the cross for your sins, and that through faith in Him, you can be forgiven. God can make your heart, your life, His home through the Holy Spirit.
3. There is something you become—a child of God.

That is the third thing—you become a child of God.

Notice it says that you don't become a child of God because of your parents. Just because they might be Jesus Followers doesn't make you one.

We always say: God has no grandchildren—only His own children.

Nor do you become a Jesus follower by your own efforts, for He says, "It is not by the will of the flesh"— that is, your flesh, what you do in your body.

There is nothing you can do, that will make God cancel your debt of sin.

Nor will you become a Christ follower because someone else makes you one. For as John says: *"Nor by the will of a man."*

That is, no other person, no matter how religious they are or what title we give them, has the power or authority to forgive your sins and make you a child of God.

Lots of people believe that because a priest or a minister baptised them when they were babies, they are Christians.

This verse in the Bible shows that this is not the case. It's not by the will of man.

This can only happen when God brings this new life about—*"you are born of God."*

This can happen to you if you believe and trust in Jesus with the commitment that you will own Him as your God and Saviour and worship Him as such.

A Defining Moment

There was one occasion when Jesus was preaching His message—you read about it in John 6—when He made one point in His message that the people realised wasn't what they wanted to hear.

So, they stood up and walked out.

Jesus then turned to His disciples and asked them: *"Are you going to leave too?"*

Peter answered: *"Lord, to whom shall we go? You have the words of eternal life."* (John 6:68)

Where Do You Stand?

This is where you find yourself right now.

You have been learning about Jesus the Teacher as we have shared His message with you. Which group will you side with?

- The ones that got up and walked away?
- Or the ones that wanted to stay and learn from God's Teacher. For Jesus is like no other person who has ever lived—and we

want to stay, engage with His teaching, so that we can know Him, the One who gives eternal life?

Jesus Is the Teacher that we Must Learn From

Jesus is:

- The Rabbi
- The Teacher
- The Master

And we all need to sit at His feet and learn how we can have salvation and then live as His citizens.

Question Time:

Here are 10 questions based on our notes: Chapter 10

1. Jesus as a Teacher – What distinguished Jesus 'teaching from that of the religious leaders of His time? How did His authority impact those who listened to Him?

2. The Authority of Jesus' Teaching – The temple guards in John 7:46 said, "No one ever spoke like this man." What does this statement reveal about the uniqueness of Jesus 'teaching?

3. The Clash Between Jesus and the Intellectuals – How does the distinction between God's wisdom and human wisdom, as described in Proverbs 3:5 and 1 Corinthians 2:14, apply to our understanding of Jesus 'message?

4. Seeking God's Wisdom – Proverbs 2:1-5 emphasises the importance of actively seeking wisdom. How does this principle relate

Identity

to Jesus' statement in John 7:17 that willingness is key to understanding His message?

5. The Real Message of Jesus – The lecture repeatedly emphasises that Jesus ' primary mission was to "seek and save the lost." How does this mission shape our understanding of His teaching and purpose?

6. Jesus and the Concept of Lostness – Many people do not recognise they are lost. Why do you think this is, and how do Jesus 'parables in Luke 15 illustrate this spiritual condition?

7. Repentance and Being Born Again – Jesus 'conversation with Nicodemus in John 3 highlights the necessity of being "born again." What does this mean, and why is it essential for entering the Kingdom of God?

8. Spiritual Blindness and Willingness to See – The chapter states, "There is no one so blind as those that don't want to see." What are some reasons people may reject Jesus 'teachings despite their evident truth?

9. Transformation Through Christ – According to 2 Corinthians 5:17-18, those in Christ become a "new creation." What are some practical signs that indicate a person has experienced this transformation?

10. Choosing to Follow the Teacher – At the end of John 6, many disciples walked away from Jesus, but Peter declared, "Lord, to whom shall we go? You have the words of eternal life." What does this response teach us about true discipleship and commitment to Jesus as our Teacher?

Al Watson

Chapter Eleven: Jesus the Messiah

The word *Christ* is the Greek word for the Hebrew word *Messiah*, so when we read *Jesus Christ* in the New Testament, we are really saying *Jesus Messiah*.

John records the interview that Jesus had with a Samaritan woman at a well in chapter 4. During the interview, and to divert the topic away from the question, "Which was the right place of worship, Samaria or Jerusalem?", the woman commented that when the Messiah comes, *"he will explain everything to us."* To which Jesus replies, *"I who speak to you am He."* (John 4:25-26)

The introduction to the coming Messiah starts in Genesis 3:15 when God addresses Satan and speaks of his destruction:

I will put enmity between you and the woman, and between your offspring and her offspring; he shall crush your head, and you shall strike his heel. (NIV)

Throughout Jewish history, people became aware that this promise of a male child coming to destroy evil, and the evil one would be special. They knew from this verse that the Messiah would be a man, the Messiah would suffer, and the Messiah would conquer; making this the Gospel in embryonic form.

1. The Messiah will be a man from the seed of a woman: a virgin birth.
2. The Messiah will suffer as the devil strikes his heel later understood as the death, burial, and resurrection of Jesus.
3. The Messiah will conquer as he crushes the devil's head.

These three gospel seeds are developed, unfolded, and explained throughout the Old Testament.

Al Watson

It is because we do not read the Old Testament as it should be read that we tend to miss so much written to reveal the coming Messiah. It was Jesus who told us how to read the Old Testament after His resurrection. Luke 24:44-47 states:

"Then he said to them, "These are my words that I spoke to you while I was still with you, that everything written about me in the Law of Moses and the Prophets, and the Psalms must be fulfilled." Then he opened their minds to understand the Scriptures, and said to them, "Thus it is written, that the Christ should suffer and on the third day rise from the dead, and that repentance for the forgiveness of sins should be proclaimed in his name to all nations, beginning from Jerusalem."

The Scriptures and Their Message

1. The Scriptures are defined as *The Law of Moses*, which consists of the first five books of the Bible; (We also include the 12 Historical books in this section) *The Prophets*, which include 17 books; and *The Psalms*, which encompass all the poetic books: Job, Psalms, Proverbs, Ecclesiastes, and the Song of Solomon. All up, 39 books.

2. The key topic to look for within the Old Testament is defined by Jesus: *"This is what is written: The Messiah will suffer and rise from the dead on the third day, and that repentance and the forgiveness of sins will be preached in His name to all nations, beginning at Jerusalem." Luke 24:46-47.*

He opened their minds so they could understand the Scriptures—meaning the Old Testament with its 39 books. The message of these books is often overlooked, but Jesus clarified that they contain the Gospel and the fulfillment of God's promise in Genesis 3:15.

The call to repentance and forgiveness is evident throughout the Old Testament. Israel, as a nation, modelled the rebellion of all mankind, and God's messengers continually called for repentance and offering

God's forgiveness through His mercy. Peter reinforced this in Acts 10:43: *"All the prophets testify about Him (Jesus) that everyone who believes in Him receives forgiveness of sins through His name."*

Seeing the Full Picture

If you were to describe a tree while standing just ten centimetres away from its trunk, you wouldn't be able to fully explain what the tree looks like. You would only see a small part of the bigger picture. The same is true when looking for Jesus in the Old Testament. We can focus so much on the personal narratives of the heroes of faith that we fail to see the overarching message behind them.

Take, for example, the promises God gave to Abraham: *Look at the stars—can you count them? Look at the sand on the seashore—can you count them?* The answer is no to both. Yet, God promised Abraham that his offspring would be innumerable. However, reality seemed different—Abraham and Sarah had no children. God could have blessed them with children early in their marriage, but He withheld this blessing until, as Hebrews 11:11 states:

"Even though he was past age—and Sarah herself was barren—was enabled to become a father because he considered Him faithful who had made the promise. And so from this one man, and he as good as dead, came descendants as numerous as the stars in the sky and as countless as the sand on the seashore."

Perhaps God was teaching something about the coming Messiah by modelling an impossible conception to take place. The birth of Isaac was miraculous, humanly speaking, preparing us to understand that the birth of God's promised Saviour would also be miraculous. Jesus, born of a virgin—the seed of a woman. The seed comes from a man, but in Jesus' case, no human male was involved in Mary's conception. His birth was entirely miraculous, *"The Word became flesh and dwelt among us."* These are the kinds of things to look for when reading the Old Testament. When you do, you will discover truths about Jesus in shadow form, foreshadowing the fulfillment of God's ultimate promise.

Much is made of the fact that the Messiah was to be King David's Greater Son. Like King David, the Messiah is presented as the conquering King. Or, as Genesis 3:15 puts it, *"He will crush Satan's head."*

Where do the origins of David's Greater Son start? It starts when David wanted to build a permanent dwelling for God, for up until this point, the tent or Tabernacle was the symbolic place where God met with His people. However, God sent a message to David through Nathan the Prophet: rather than David building a house for God, God was going to establish an eternal dynasty for the house of David. You read this in 2 Samuel 7.

We know that David was not allowed to be the builder of the Temple:

"But God said to me, 'You may not build a house for my name, for you are a man of war and have shed blood.'" 2 Chronicles 28:3.

This task was given to Solomon, David's son.

But when you read Nathan's relayed message from God, you will see that Solomon could not be the only person being spoken of. For we read: *"When your days are fulfilled and you lie down with your fathers, I will raise up your offspring after you, who shall come from your body, and I will establish his kingdom. He shall build a house for my name* (this is obviously speaking about Solomon) *and I will establish the throne of his kingdom forever."* (But this cannot be speaking about Solomon's sons, who came to the throne after Solomon's death.)

"...Your throne shall be established forever."

When you read the account of the message given to both Mary and her husband Joseph, you will notice that the angel refers to the family line of David and that Jesus was to be the fulfillment of the promise given to David—that he would have an heir on the throne forever.

Message to Joseph Matthew 1:20-23

"But as he considered these things, behold, an angel of the Lord appeared to him in a dream, saying, 'Joseph, son of David, do not fear to take Mary as your wife, for that which is conceived in her is from the Holy Spirit. She will bear a son, and you shall call his name Jesus, for he will save his people from their sins.' All this took place to fulfill what the Lord had spoken by the prophet: 'Behold, the virgin shall conceive and bear a son, and they shall call his name Immanuel' (which means, God with us).

Message to Mary Luke 1:26-27, 31-33

"In the sixth month, the angel Gabriel was sent from God to a city of Galilee named Nazareth, to a virgin betrothed to a man whose name was Joseph, of the house of David. And the virgin's name was Mary."

"And behold, you will conceive in your womb and bear a son, and you shall call his name Jesus. He will be great and will be called the Son of the Most High. And the Lord God will give to him the throne of his father David, and he will reign over the house of Jacob forever, and of his kingdom, there will be no end."

It is interesting to notice that when Jesus was born, there were godly people already looking for and expecting the birth of the Messiah—people like Simeon and Anna. Their story is found in Luke 2:22-38.

So why would they have been looking for and expecting the birth of the Messiah?

The answer is in the revelation God gave to Daniel, for in Daniel 9, we find the timeline given for the coming of the Messiah. There was also another prophet who spoke of the exact events that would take place on the day the Messiah presented Himself to Israel as their King—and that was Zechariah (9:9). *"Rejoice greatly, O daughter of Zion! Shout aloud, O daughter of Jerusalem! Behold, your king is coming to you; righteous and having salvation is he, humble and mounted on a donkey, on a colt, the foal of a donkey."* We know this is what Christians call Palm Sunday. The record of this event is found in Matthew 21:1-11.

It was Daniel who gave the date the Messiah would come. With a little investigation, you can see how accurate this promised presentation of the Messiah was. You will also see how Jesus was rejected by His own people as stated in this prophesy.

When we read chapter nine, we see that Daniel was only asking God to fulfill His promise to Jeremiah, that this, the captivity in Babylon would only last for 70 years. Why 70 years? Because the nation failed to keep the Sabbath rest for the land. (Leviticus 25:5) This is what 2 Chronicles 36:21 indicates. *"to fulfill the word of the LORD by the mouth of Jeremiah, until the land had enjoyed its Sabbaths. All the days that it lay desolate it kept Sabbath, to fulfill seventy years."*.

However Daniel received much more that he asked for. Daniel was told when the Messiah would come. As we read this, (Daniel 9:24-27 (NIV) remember the word "week" is also the word for "seven" in Hebrew.

Daniel's Prophecy of the Seventy 'Sevens' and the Coming of the Messiah

"Seventy 'sevens' are decreed for your people and your holy city to finish transgression, to put an end to sin, to atone for wickedness, to bring in everlasting righteousness, to seal up vision and prophecy, and to anoint the Most Holy Place." (Daniel 9:24)

While the phrase *"to anoint the Most Holy Place"* has been the subject of much scholarly debate, the rest of the prophecy unmistakably points to what Jesus accomplished through His death and resurrection.

The term *"seventy sevens"* refers to seventy sets of seven years—490 years in total. These 490 years are divided into two primary segments: one of 483 years and another of 7 years.

The Timeline

Daniel gives a cryptic breakdown:

- The first 7 'sevens' = 49 years
- Followed by 62 'sevens' = 434 years
- Together they total 483 years

There is no indication of a gap between these periods in the original prophecy. So the key question becomes: **When does the clock start ticking?**

Daniel 9:25 tells us: *"From the time the word goes out to restore and rebuild Jerusalem..."*

This decree was issued by the Persian King Artaxerxes, as recorded in Ezra 7:11–26. The date of this edict is believed to be **457 BC**.

Now, if we begin counting from 457 BC and go forward 483 years, we arrive at **AD 26**. But this is approximately **seven years short** of the commonly accepted year of Jesus' crucifixion—**AD 33**. So where are the missing years?

The Calendar Adjustment

The answer lies in the difference between the **Jewish lunar calendar** and our modern **solar calendar**. The Jewish year had **360 days**, compared to the 365 days of the Gregorian solar calendar.

Calculating the difference:

- 483 years × 5 extra days/year = 2,415 extra days
- 2,415 days ÷ 360 days/year = roughly **6.7 years**

Adding this to AD 26 brings us close to **AD 33**, the year many scholars place the crucifixion. While we must be cautious about asserting exact dates, the prophecy provides a compelling timeframe that would have prompted the people of Jesus' day to expect the arrival of the Messiah.

Al Watson

The Messiah Will Be Cut Off

Daniel 9:26 says: *"After the sixty-two 'sevens,' the Anointed One will be put to death and will have nothing."* This is a clear prophecy about the death of the Messiah.

At the time of Jesus, many religious groups were actively expecting the Messiah. One such group—the **Herodians**—believed King Herod was the promised one, based on their reading of Daniel's prophecy. *Mark 3:6* – *"Then the Pharisees went out and began to plot with the Herodians how they might kill Jesus."*

Even John the Baptist was momentarily thought to be the Messiah: *John 1:19–20* – *"Now this was John's testimony when the Jewish leaders in Jerusalem sent priests and Levites to ask him who he was. He did not fail to confess, but confessed freely, 'I am not the Messiah.'"*

Palm Sunday and the Fulfilment of Prophecy

Daniel's prophecy indicated that the Messiah would appear as King at the end of the 483 years. This aligns with **Jesus' triumphal entry into Jerusalem**, riding on a donkey's colt.

This moment was prophesied by Zechariah over 400 years earlier: *Zechariah 9:9* – *"Rejoice greatly, O daughter of Zion! ... Behold, your king is coming to you; righteous and having salvation is he, humble and mounted on a donkey..."*

If this isn't evidence of divine inspiration, then what is?

Luke's Gospel records the people's joyful response as they welcomed Jesus as King: *Luke 19:35–40* – *"Blessed is the King who comes in the name of the Lord!"* But when the Pharisees objected, Jesus replied, *"If they keep quiet, the stones will cry out."*

Jesus then wept over Jerusalem, foretelling its destruction, because, as He said: *"You did not recognise the time of God's coming to you."* (Luke 19:44)

They were living in the very days foretold by Daniel—but because Jesus did not match their expectations, they rejected Him.

Condemned for Truth

At His trial, the high priest demanded Jesus declare whether He was the Messiah:
Matthew 26:63–66 – "Tell us if you are the Messiah..." Jesus replied, "You have said so... From now on you will see the Son of Man sitting at the right hand of the Mighty One..." This was enough for them to condemn Him for blasphemy.

However, since they lacked authority to carry out capital punishment, Jesus was handed over to the Romans. This fulfilled the prophecy of His **death by crucifixion**.

Jesus and the Cross Foretold

Jesus had already told Nicodemus: *John 3:14–15 – "Just as Moses lifted up the snake in the wilderness, so the Son of Man must be lifted up..."* He would be lifted up on the Cross—just as Daniel had foretold centuries earlier.

Had the people studied Daniel 9 carefully, they would have seen it clearly: *"After the sixty-two 'sevens,' the Anointed One will be put to death and will have nothing."*

It is called the 62 'sevens,' but it includes the earlier 7 'sevens'—making the full 483 years leading up to His death.

Peter's Summary

1 Peter 1:10–12 – "Concerning this salvation, the prophets... searched intently... trying to find out the time and circumstances... when He predicted the sufferings of the Messiah and the glories that would follow... Even angels long to look into these things."

The Final Seven Years

Many Bible teachers believe that the final seven years—the last "week" of Daniel's prophecy—remains unfulfilled. This final period, yet to come, is viewed as another mountain peak in the distance. I am among those who hold this view

The Final Seven – A Matter of Interpretation

Many Bible teachers believe that the final "week" — the last seven years of Daniel's 70-week prophecy — still awaits future fulfilment. This period is seen as another prophetic mountain peak in the distance, possibly relating to the end times. I personally hold to this view.

However, there are also respected Bible scholars who argue that all seventy weeks were fulfilled within the first century of the Christian Church. They point out that the entirety of Daniel's prophecy finds its fulfilment in the life, death, resurrection, and early impact of Jesus and the Church. A thoughtful and compelling presentation of this view can be found in Rodney Stortz's commentary on Daniel, part of the *Preach the Word* series.

Both views seek to honour the integrity of Scripture and the centrality of Christ in prophecy, and while interpretations may vary, the core truth remains unshaken: Jesus is the Messiah whom Daniel foretold.

This is only one of the many main themes that introduce Jesus as the Messiah. The Old Testament contains many more.

If you remove all the repeated promises (of which there are around 200), such as references to the Messiah coming from King David's family,

Identity

you still find 109 references to the coming Messiah in the 39 books of the Old Testament.

Time does not permit us to look at them all, but let's take a quick look at some key ones:

Old Testament Prophecies of the Messiah

1. His birthplace

Micah 5:1-2 foretold it.
This is what King Herod was told when the wise men from the east came looking for Jesus.
Matthew 2:6, compared with John 7:42.

2. The coming prophet like Moses

Deuteronomy 18:18—God told Moses that He would raise up a prophet like him.
People frequently asked Jesus if He was that prophet:

John 6:14, John 7:40-41.

3. Jesus would come out of Egypt

Hosea 11:1—Matthew referred to this to show that Jesus would come out of Egypt. Matthew 2:13-15.

Isaiah's many prophetic indicators :
1. Virgin birth – Isaiah 7:14.
2. The cause for many to stumble – Isaiah 8:14; 1 Peter 2:8.
3. A child is born, but a son is given – Isaiah 9:6. This means He already existed so that He could be given.
4. The sure foundation – Isaiah 28:16.
Peter tells us this was a reference to Jesus – 1 Peter 2:8.
5. The suffering Messiah – Isaiah 53.

Al Watson

Messianic Psalms

Psalm 2 – The political rulers seek to condemn the LORD and His Messiah (Anointed One).

Matthew 27:1, Acts 13:33, Hebrews 1:5.

Psalm 16 – The resurrection of Jesus (v.10).

Quoted in Acts 2:24-32, Acts 13:34-37.

Psalm 22 – The crucified Messiah.

This psalm describes crucifixion centuries before it was historically known (v.16).

Psalm 69 – The Messiah cleanses the Temple (v.9). John 2.

He would be given sour wine for His thirst. (v21) John 19:28-29. Judas would be replaced (v25) Acts 1:20 and Psalm 109:8

Psalm 110 – The most quoted Psalm in the New Testament.

The Ultimate Message

The list goes on and on and on because the Old Testament was written to reveal countless truths about Jesus, the Messiah—so that when He came, He would be recognised.

But was He?

Sadly, many were blind to the truth, and today things are not much different. Most people ignore the many "convincing proofs" that Jesus is the Messiah.

Identity

Question Time: Here are 10 questions based on our notes: Chapter 11

1. The Meaning of Christ and Messiah
How does understanding that "Christ" means "Messiah" influence our reading of the New Testament?

2. The Samaritan Woman's Expectation of the Messiah
What does the conversation between Jesus and the Samaritan woman in John 4 reveal about first-century Jewish and Samaritan expectations of the Messiah?

3. Genesis 3:15 and the Gospel in Embryonic Form
How does Genesis 3:15 lay the foundation for the Gospel message, and how do we see its fulfilment in Jesus?

4. Jesus 'Explanation of the Old Testament
Why did Jesus need to "open the minds" of His disciples to understand the Old Testament after His resurrection (Luke 24:44-47)?

5. Messianic Themes in the Old Testament
What are some ways the Old Testament foreshadows Jesus as the Messiah, and why do people often miss these connections?

6. The Miraculous Births of Isaac and Jesus
How does the miraculous birth of Isaac help prepare us to understand the virgin birth of Jesus?

7. God's Promise to David and Its Fulfilment
What is the significance of God's promise to David in 2 Samuel 7, and how is it ultimately fulfilled in Jesus?

8. Daniel's Prophecy and the Timeline of the Messiah
How does Daniel's prophecy (Daniel 9:24-27) provide a timeline for the coming of the Messiah, and how does it align with Jesus 'life and death?

Al Watson

9. Messianic Prophecies and Their Fulfilment in Jesus
Which specific Old Testament prophecies about the Messiah stand out to you the most, and why?

10. Recognising the Messiah Today
If Jesus fulfilled so many prophecies, why did many in His time—and many today—fail to recognise Him as the Messiah?

Identity

Al Watson

Chapter Twelve : Jesus The Son of God

The next two titles—**Son of God** and **King of Israel**—frequently appear together in the New Testament. Along with the final title, **Son of Man**, all three are brought together in the conversation Jesus has with Nathanael in **John 1:45–51**. It was Philip who found Nathanael and announced that they had found the Messiah. However, when Philip mentioned that Jesus was from Nazareth, Nathanael's sceptical reply revealed his prejudice: *"Can anything good come from there?"*

But his attitude changed dramatically after a brief encounter with Jesus. The turning point came when Jesus revealed that He already knew intimate details about Nathanael—specifically, that he was sitting under a fig tree when Philip invited him to meet the Teacher. Jesus' insight convinced Nathanael that this was no ordinary man. Jesus recognised the sincerity of Nathanael's heart, and in response, Nathanael declared: *"You are the Son of God; you are the King of Israel."*

It's clear that Nathanael was deeply moved by Jesus' words because he knew Jesus *couldn't* have seen him under the fig tree by natural means—he hadn't been anywhere nearby. So how could Jesus have known where he was? And more significantly, how could Jesus declare, *"Here truly is an Israelite in whom there is no deceit"*? What prompted such a statement?

This wasn't a surface-level observation—it pointed to something deeper. Jesus seemed to know not only where Nathanael had been, but what he had been *thinking* about. Many scholars and Bible teachers believe that Nathanael had been meditating under the fig tree on the life of **Jacob**, the patriarch who had deceived his brother *twice*, yet was still chosen by God to become the father of the twelve tribes. God eventually changed his name to **Israel**, the very name that defines the people of God.

Identity

In this brief but powerful exchange, Jesus reveals His divine insight, confirms Nathanael's faith, and hints at even greater revelations to come.

If this is all true, and we believe it fits the facts, it's little wonder Nathanael reached the conclusion that Jesus is the Messiah and is therefore the Son of God and the rightful King of Israel. It is not asking too much to assume that Nathanael had a keen understanding of his Scriptures. Therefore, he would have known that the second Psalm reveals the titles given to the coming promised Messiah, for it shows that the Messiah is both the Son of God and the King of Israel.

"Why do the nations rage and the peoples plot in vain? The kings of the earth set themselves, and the rulers take counsel together, against the LORD and against his Anointed, saying," There is the first title, for the word *"Anointed"* is the word "Messiah" in Hebrew, and "Christ" in Greek.

In verse 4, God's response is given to the kings of the earth: *"He who sits in the heavens laughs; the Lord holds them in derision."* Then in verse 6, God tells the kings of the earth that He has set His King in Jerusalem: *"As for me, I have set my King on Zion, my holy hill."* (Zion is what Jerusalem was called when King David conquered it, 2 Samuel 5:6-7, and it has retained both names throughout the Scriptures.)

Now we have the first mention that God will establish His King's reign in Jerusalem, and Jesus is that King. Then, in verse 7, God reveals that the King is God the Son: *"I will tell of the decree: The LORD said to me, 'You are my Son...'"* It is the Son of God that will be King.

There we have the two names which are often linked simultaneously in Scripture: Son of God and King of Israel.

However, each require their own fuller investigation as to how they apply to Jesus. The name *Jesus* is associated with the human person of Jesus, whereas the title *Son of God* defines His divinity.

This is *Immanuel – God with us* (Isaiah 7:14). We know that Jesus is called *the Word*, and we know that *the Word was with God and is God*. John 1:1-2. It is clear from Scripture that the person of Jesus, who is God the Son come in the flesh to dwell among mankind, is presented to us as a member of the Triune Godhead, for it says:

- *He is God manifest in the flesh* (1 Timothy 3:16).
- *He is in the form of God* (Philippians 2:6-8).
- *He is the exact representation of God's nature* (Hebrews 1:1-3).
- Jesus said, *"If you have seen Me, you have seen the Father"* (John 14:9).
- *"And the Word became flesh and dwelt among us, and we have seen his glory, glory as of the only Son from the Father, full of grace and truth."* (John 1:14.)

Not only are these claims made of Jesus, but they are also backed up by His actions. He did things that humans cannot do:

- He raised people who had been dead for up to four days (John 11).
- He restored the sight of blind people (John 9).
- He walked on the Sea of Galilee to catch up with His disciples who were in a boat (John 6:16-21).
- He fed 5,000 men with only *"five barley loaves and two small fish"*, which kept multiplying in His hands as He distributed the food to His disciples for them to give to the masses. They then filled 12 baskets with the leftovers (John 6:9,13).

These are just a few examples of what Doctor Luke called *"many convincing proofs"* (Acts 1:3), proving that Jesus was not just human—He is the Son of God. For this reason, He said, *"Believe me that I am in the Father and the Father is in me, or else believe on account of the works themselves."* (John 14:11).

From Jesus 'point of self-disclosure, there was no ambiguity. He revealed to the religious leaders in John 14:11 they should have identified Him by His medicals.

Who is this Son of God? Can He be Known? Where did He Come From?

There are things about the Godhead that are beyond our understanding. No wonder Paul said:

"Oh, the depths of the riches of the wisdom and the knowledge of God! How unsearchable his judgments and his paths beyond tracing out." – Romans 11:33

What did Paul mean by *his paths beyond tracing out*? It means that if you follow any characteristic of God's nature or actions with the desire to understand it fully, you will never finish the search—there is just no end to your pursuit of discovery.

But don't take that to mean that we should not try to understand what God has revealed. He is the God of revelation, a God who communicates so that we might know Him. Remember what Jesus said in John 17:3 *"And this is eternal life, that they know you, the only true God, and Jesus Christ whom you have sent."*

The Titles of the Triune God

Have you ever thought about the titles of the triune God—God the Father, God the Son, and God the Holy Spirit? How did God the Father become the Father, and when did God the Son become the Son that the Father loves? How does the Holy Spirit relate to the Father and the Son?

I became a father on May 10th, 1972, when my first son was born. It was the birth of my child that made me a father. So, does that mean that there was a time when God the Son didn't exist? We know that is not the case, for God is eternal. Isaiah 9:6 speaks about the everlasting Father, therefor that means the Son must be everlasting. Hebrews 7:3 – speaking of Melchizedek (as a type of Christ): *"He is without father or mother or genealogy, having neither beginning of days nor end of life, but resembling the Son of God he continues a priest forever."* So how do we understand the relationship between the Father, Son, and Holy Spirit?

Think of it this way: there is God, God, God—three, yet one. Now, a decision was made, for reasons known to the Godhead, that three titles would be adopted. One would assume the role and title and responsibilities of Father, one would assume the role and title and responsibilities of Son, and one would assume the title and role and responsibilities of the Holy Spirit.

None had a greater role or a lesser role than the other—they simply took the responsibility of acting in these different roles. No illustration fully explains the triune Godhead, but we know that God—Father, Son, and Holy Spirit—is a *consuming fire* (Hebrews 12:29). There are three things that make up fire: fuel, heat, and oxygen. Each of these stands by itself, but all three together are what constitutes fire.

In this study we want to understand who the Son of God is.

The Narrative of Creation and Redemption

To do this, we need to go back to the narrative of creation and the severed relationship with God caused by man's sinful rebellion and rejection. Remember, mankind was created in God's image to be His image-bearer. We also have the will of God the Father to save the rebels, but that salvation would need to be carried out in a way that upheld the holy character of God while displaying mercy, grace, and love.

It is revealed that the Son volunteered to carry out this saving work. The record comes in Psalm 40:7. *"Then I said, "Behold, I have come; in the scroll of the book it is written of me: I delight to do your will, O my God; your law is within my heart."*

Some Psalms are classified as *Messianic Psalms*, which means there is a backstory to what you read—something greater than just the narrative. This backstory is a revelation of the coming Messiah, Jesus Christ, the Son of God. We know this is true of Psalm 40 because the Holy Spirit, in His revelation of the New Testament book of Hebrews, applies this verse to Jesus: *"Therefore, when Christ came into the world, he said, 'Sacrifice and offerings you did not desire, but a body you prepared for me; with burnt offerings* and sin offerings you were not pleased. Then I said, Here I am—it is written about me in the scroll—I have come to do your will, my God.'" – Hebrews 10:5-7

This Psalm is not just about King David who wrote it; it is really about Christ, using David's experiences and words to reflect the mind and will of God the Son. He was the one willing to come and become the saving sacrifice. *"Sacrifice and offerings you did not desire, but a body you prepared for me;"*

It is the Son of God who makes the statement about all the Old Testament sacrifices. In verse 6, He speaks of four sacrifices that refer to the Levitical offerings for sin, then declares that God did not require them.

By that, Jesus means that the Old Testament sacrifices could never bring true forgiveness for the one making the offering. They only carried two messages—that what is about to happen to this animal should be happening to you and one day, a perfect sacrifice would come and procure the means of forgiveness. The Son of God would be the promised perfect sacrifice.

This, of course, was fulfilled through the death of Jesus on the cross, where Isaiah the prophet says: *"... He was pierced for our transgressions; He was crushed for our iniquities; upon Him was the judgment that brought us peace, and with His wounds, we are healed. All we like sheep have gone astray; we have turned—everyone—to his own way; and the LORD has laid on Him the iniquity of us all."* – Isaiah 53:4-6.

The Sacrificial Death of the Son of God

How can we process this?

The Son of God became a man so that He might die a death unlike any other. Who would do that? Who would subject themselves to a mocked trial, be flogged to the extent that their back resembled the furrows of a ploughed field?

Then, to be nailed through His hands and feet by Roman soldiers to a cross, lifted up, and dropped into the hole that kept the cross erect. For three gruelling hours, He was mocked by the very people dependent on Him for the very breath in their lungs.

Endured the sarcastic comments hurled at Him: "*If you are the Son of God, come down off the cross! You saved others, but you can't even save yourself.*" If only they knew!

Then, at high noon, a supernatural darkness enveloped the area. During that time, the Son of God endured the judgment for all the people in the history of this world—those who had lived in the past and those yet to live—who would and had believed in the salvation that God the Father sent the Son to make possible. He said, "*I will suffer many things and be rejected by the elders and the chief priests and the scribes and be killed, and after three days rise again.*" Mark 8:31

This was why He can now say,

- *I am the way.*
- *I am the truth.*
- *I am the life. No one can come to God except through me*
- *I am the door by me if anyone enters in you will be saved*
- *I am the true vine abide in me and your life will be fruitful.*

This is the Son of God that loves you and gave His life for you: now we are asking you to believe in Him. The one who said,

- *This is my blood of the new covenant, which is shed for many for the forgiveness of sin.*
- *I am the resurrection and the life.*
- *I am the light of the world.*

    I am from above.

- *I have come down from heaven.*

- *Before Abraham was, I AM. If you do not believe that I AM, you will die in your sins.*
- *All power is given to me in heaven and on earth.*

I AM greater than the temple.

- *A greater than Solomon is here.*
- *A greater than Jonah is here.*
- *I am the Lord of the Sabbath.*
- *He who has seen me has seen the Father.*
- *Come to me, all you who labour and are heavy laden, and I will give you rest.*
- *You call me Master and Lord, and that is true, for so I am.*
- *Heaven and earth shall pass away, but my words shall not pass away.*
- *You shall see the Son of Man sitting on the right hand of power and coming in the clouds of heaven.*
- *The Son of Man shall come, and then He will reward every man according to his works.*

Until then,

- *I am with you always, even unto the end of the world.*

No wonder they said, "*No man ever spoke like this man*", that was because there has never been a man like this man, this is the God Man, the Eternal Divine Son of God.

These are the words of the Son of God.

They would be blasphemous if they did not come from the very lips of Him who is the *Great I AM*—the name given by God to reveal Himself to Moses in Exodus 3. Which is the name Jesus applied to Himself eight times in John's Gospel.

If a human made those claims, we would question their sanity. To a religious Jew, if someone made these claims they would be stoned to death for blasphemy—which was attempted against Jesus multiple times:

- *"This was why the Jews were seeking all the more to kill him, because not only was he breaking the Sabbath, but he was even calling God his own Father, making himself equal with God."* (John 5:18)

However, He was not destined to die from stoning. It was prophesied that He would die on a cross. He told the chief teacher of Israel, Nicodemus that *"Just as Moses lifted up the serpent in the wilderness, so must the Son of Man be lifted up"*. John 3:14.

The Necessity of the God-Man

The reason we needed the Son of God to take humanity into His divine being was the cross. There had to be a man because it was the first man who brought sin into the world, and he and all his descendants faced the consequences—God's judgment and the second death.

But no ordinary man could endure that. This is why it had to be the God-Man—for only He could endure the wrath of the justice of God, and only a man could experience death.

Have you recognised who He is?

Do you believe in Him in such a way that you totally trust Him and live under His protection, resting in the perfect peace He gives? Has He become your greatest treasure, evident in how you revolve your life around His will?

Have you received Him and embraced Him?

If so, you have been born of God, and to use the Apostle Paul's words, *you have passed out of the kingdom of darkness into the kingdom of the Son that God loves* (Colossians 1:13). You are now part of His eternal family—a child of God.

Identity

So now, this new life journey begins. He leads, we follow, and as a babe in Christ, it starts with three things:

1. Baptism – When a person dies, they are buried. You have died in Christ, so you need to experience the waters of baptism, the symbol of your burial and resurrection in to new life that you have received by faith in Christ.

"Having been buried with him in baptism, in which you were also raised with him through faith in the powerful working of God, who raised him from the dead." (Colossians 2:12). This is how you reenact your spiritual death, burial, and resurrection to new life. Baptism does not give you new life in Christ; rather, it is a symbolic act that dramatises the transformation that is already taken place within you.

2. The Word of God – You need what the Apostle called the "milk of the word":

"Like newborn infants, long for the pure spiritual milk, that by it you may grow up into salvation—if indeed you have tasted that the Lord is good." (1 Peter 2:2-3)

Start by reading through John's Gospel and read it many times until you know what it says and where to find the stories that carry the message of the Gospel.

3. Sharing the Good News – Begin doing what Jesus told a new follower:

"Go home to your friends and tell them how much the Lord has done for you, and how he has had mercy on you." (Mark 5:1-20)

This is the same thing Peter said we should do:

"That you may proclaim the excellencies of him who called you out of darkness into his marvellous light." (1 Peter 2:9).

Here are 10 questions based on our notes: Chapter 12.

1. What significance do the titles "Son of God" and "King of Israel" hold in relation to Jesus, particularly in His conversation with Nathanael in John 1:45-51?

2. How does Jesus' reference to Jacob's dream (Genesis 28:12) connect with Nathanael's recognition of Jesus as the Messiah?

3. What evidence from Scripture and Jesus' own words confirm His divinity and His role in the Triune Godhead?

4. How do Jesus' miracles, such as raising the dead and walking on water, support His identity as the Son of God?

5. What is the theological significance of Jesus volunteering to become the perfect sacrifice as foretold in Psalm 40 and fulfilled in Hebrews 10?

6. Why was Jesus' sacrificial death necessary, and how does it fulfill Old Testament prophecies such as Isaiah 53?

7. How does Jesus 'role as the God-Man uniquely qualify Him to bridge the gap between God's holiness and human sinfulness?

8. What does it mean to "receive" and "embrace" Jesus as the Son of God, and how does that transform a believer's life?

9. How do baptism, studying Scripture, and sharing the Gospel serve as foundational steps for new believers in their faith journey?

10. What does Jesus' statement, "I am the way, the truth, and the life" (John 14:6), reveal about the exclusivity of salvation through Him?

Identity

Chapter Thirteen: Jesus The King of Israel

There is a great song written by Jeremy Riddle in 2017 that captures the key thoughts behind this title, King of Israel. Jesus is called the "The King of Love" and then there is this great anthem

All hail King Jesus

All hail the Lord of Heaven and Earth

All hail King Jesus

All hail the Saviour of the world.

When you study the history of Israel, you find that it was a **treasonous act** that set the first king on the throne. **Treason** is the unlawful overthrow of a ruling king. In their case, **God was their King**..

The people were led by what became known as **Judges**. The last to lead was **Samuel**. It was typical for the judgeship to be handed down to the next generation of the judge's family. However, Samuel's sons were known to be corrupt, so the people demanded that they become like all the surrounding nations and appoint a king to lead the nation.

The record is found in **1 Samuel 8:4–7**: *"Then all the elders of Israel gathered together and came to Samuel at Ramah and said to him, 'Behold, you are old, and your sons do not walk in your ways. Now appoint for us a king to judge us like all the nations.' But the thing displeased Samuel when they said, 'Give us a king to judge us.' And Samuel prayed to the LORD. And the LORD said to Samuel, 'Obey the voice of the people in all that they say to you, for they have not rejected you, but they have rejected me from being king over them.'"*

Identity

Over the next 120 years, three kings ruled Israel: Saul, David, and Solomon. Then Solomon's son Rehoboam came to the throne (*1 Kings 12*). The unwise decisions he made led to a schism. Ten tribes seceded and appointed Jeroboam as their king. This marked the beginning of the demise of the ten northern tribes of Israel.

Over the next **330 years**, under **19 kings**, not one of them governed with **Godly values**.

It is always interesting to note that God does not value a nation based on their GDP or their military might, or its population size but they're always valued on whether they did evil in the sight of God or good in the eyes of God.

We know that Samuel was, *"displeased …when they said, "Give us a king to judge us." And Samuel prayed to the LORD."* However, God's answer is very revealing for this is why we call these events treasonous. The people were overthrowing the rightful king.

".. they have not rejected you, but they have rejected me from being king over them."

Israel was always a Theocracy, God was their King, now He was rejected and dethroned.

Despite what man will do, God can always bring good out of mans sinful actions. You see this in the words of Joseph when speaking to his brothers who had sold him as a slave at 17 years of age out of jealousy. Yet Joseph saw past that and said to them, *"you meant evil against me, but God meant it for good, to bring it about that many people should be kept alive, as they are today"*. (Genesis 50:20).

Israels first king was Saul, yet he failed to live up to the privilege given him. However, the second king was David and despite the failures in his life, at heart he always wanted to please God. The Apostle Paul in one of his sermons had this to say about King David. *"And when he had removed him (King Saul), he raised up David to be their king, of whom he testified and said, 'I have found in David the son of Jesse a man after my heart, who will do all my will. 'Of this man's offspring God has brought to Israel a Savior, Jesus, as he promised" (Acts13:22-23).*

When you read the covenant that God made with King David, you will see woven into that covenant the promise that one day there will be David's Greater Son. For David's son Solomon, next in line to the throne, could never fulfil all that is revealed.

2 Samuel 7:12-14

"When your days are fulfilled and you lie down with your fathers, I will raise up your offspring after you, who shall come from your body, and I will establish his kingdom. He shall build a house for my name, and I will establish the throne of his kingdom forever."

There is more here than just King Solomon. While Solomon built the temple, or *"the house for my name,"* his kingdom did not last forever, nor did the temple. So, there is someone else within these words, and it is Jesus.

As David's Greater Son, Jesus will reign forever—not only as King of Israel but as King of Kings and Lord of Lords. This was told to Mary by the angel:

Luke 1:32-33 Speaking about Jesus, *"He will be great and will be called the Son of the Most High. And the Lord God will give to him the throne of his father David, and he will reign over the house of Jacob forever, and of his kingdom there will be no end."*

Then these is Isaiah the prophet.

Isaiah 9:6-7

"For to us a child is born, to us a son is given; and the government shall be upon his shoulder, and his name shall be called Wonderful Counsellor, Mighty God, Everlasting Father, Prince of Peace. Of the increase of his government and of peace there will be no end, on the throne of David and over his kingdom, to establish it

and to uphold it with justice and with righteousness from this time forth and forevermore. The zeal of the Lord of hosts will do this."

1. The child is Born but the Son is given which implies that the Son already existed
2. Mighty God is also revealed as having an eternal Son
3. The King will rule His Kingdom.

The Davidic Covenant

The Davidic Covenant (2 Samuel 7:4-17; 1 Chronicles 17:3-15) was an unconditional covenant in which God promised David an everlasting royal lineage, a throne, and a kingdom—each enduring forever. While God retained the right to interrupt the actual reign of David's successors when discipline was necessary (2 Samuel 7:14-15; Psalm 89:20-37), the perpetuity of the covenant itself remains unbroken.

Just as the Abrahamic Covenant guaranteed Israel's eternal status as a nation (Jeremiah 31:36) and their everlasting possession of the land (Genesis 13:15; 1 Chronicles 16:15-18; Psalm 105:9-11), the Davidic Covenant assured them of:

An everlasting throne (2 Samuel 7:16; Psalm 89:36),

An everlasting king (Jeremiah 33:21), and

An everlasting kingdom (Daniel 7:14).

From the moment this covenant was established and confirmed by God's oath (Acts 2:30), until the birth of Christ, David never lacked a descendant to sit on his throne (Jeremiah 33:21). Christ, the Eternal Son of God and son of David, is the rightful heir to this throne. One day, He will sit upon it, fulfilling God's promise that David's lineage would endure forever (Luke 1:31-33).

The Fulfilment of the Davidic Covenant.

Al Watson

The Davidic Covenant is central to the millennial kingdom, in which Christ will reign on earth (Revelation 20:1-3; Isaiah 2:4). During this period, the resurrected David will serve under Christ as a prince over Israel (Ezekiel 34:23-24; 37:24).

This covenant is not fulfilled by Christ sitting on His Father's throne in heaven, and David never sat—nor will ever sit—on the Father's throne. Moreover, the millennium is not a figurative period spanning from Christ's resurrection to His Second Coming. Rather, God's promises require a literal earthly throne and kingdom. These will be established after Christ's return, during His 1,000-year reign, and will culminate in the final Great White Throne Judgment (Revelation 20:11-15).

As Jesus Himself declared: *"When the Son of Man comes in His glory, and all the angels with Him, then He will sit on His glorious throne."* (Matthew 25:31)

This event has not yet taken place. It will be fulfilled after Jesus returns to save Israel from annihilation. As foretold by Zechariah, at that time, Israel will experience a deep spiritual awakening:

"I will pour out on the house of David and the inhabitants of Jerusalem a spirit of grace and pleas for mercy, so that, when they look on Me, on Him whom they have pierced, they shall mourn for Him, as one mourns for an only child, and weep bitterly over Him, as one weeps over a firstborn." (Zechariah 12:10)

The rejected King—Jesus, who first came to save—will finally be received as Israel's Messiah. He will be worshipped as God, fulfilling His divine role as the King of Israel.

The Act of Treason affects us all, for we have all said—like the nation of Israel at the Cross—*"We will not have this man to reign over us."* But that treasonous act has been **dealt with** for all who will believe—**on the Cross.**

When the Roman Empire crucified a person, they would place a written reason for the capital punishment on a plaque and nail it to the cross. On the cross above the head of Jesus were the words: **"King of the**

Jews." Little did they know the truth behind this statement. For the **Son of God died to pay the judgment price** for our spiritual treason—the sin of rejecting the King of Kings and Lord of Lords—of all who would believe in Him.

Al Watson

Here are 10 questions based on the lecture: Chapter 13

1. "Israel's Rejection of God as King": In 1 Samuel 8, Israel demanded a human king, rejecting God's rule. How do we see similar patterns of rejecting God's leadership in modern society or personal lives?

2. "The Role of Kingship in God's Plan": Despite Israel's rejection of God as King, He used human kings to ultimately bring about the Messiah. How does this show God's sovereignty in working through human failures?

3. "Lessons from Saul and David": Saul and David had very different leadership styles and relationships with God. What lessons can we learn from their reigns about leadership and faithfulness to God?

4. "David as a "Man After God's Own Heart": Acts 13:22 describes David as a man after God's heart. What does this mean, and how can we apply this concept to our own lives?

5. "The Davidic Covenant": In 2 Samuel 7, God promises David that his throne will last forever. How is this ultimately fulfilled in Jesus Christ?

6. "Jesus as the True King": In Luke 1:32-33, the angel tells Mary that Jesus will reign over an eternal kingdom. What does this mean for believers today?

7. "The Prophetic Role of Isaiah": Isaiah 9:6-7 describes Jesus as "Wonderful Counsellor, Mighty God, Everlasting Father, Prince of Peace." How do these titles help us understand Jesus 'mission and character?

8. "Israel's Recognition of Jesus as King": Zechariah 12:10 predicts a time when Israel will recognize the Messiah they once rejected. How does this prophecy relate to future events in biblical eschatology?

Identity

9. "God's Covenant Promises": The Davidic Covenant assures an eternal throne, kingdom, and king. How does understanding this covenant impact our faith in God's promises?

10. "Jesus 'Future Reign": Revelation 20 speaks of Jesus 'millennial reign. How should the promise of Christ's future kingship influence the way we live today?

Al Watson

Chapter Fourteen: Jesus The Son of Man

The Son of Man in John's Gospel

The term Son of Man is used 13 times in John's Gospel and over 80 times across all the Gospels. So, what does this name or title mean? Sometimes, it is simply a substitute for "I", but mostly, it is used in relation to the upcoming suffering of Christ in procuring salvation for the lost. It then looks forward beyond the resurrection to the glory that will be given to Him. The name is drawn from Daniel 7:13, which we will look at later.

The Three Responsibilities of Jesus, the Son of Man

Jesus, the Son of Man, is revealed as having three responsibilities as the Son of Man:

1. He is to be the Judge of mankind after the resurrection of the dead.
2. He is to be crucified so that whoever believes in Him will be saved.
3. He is to enter the full restoration of His glory and bring His redeemed into that glory.

The Setting of This Title

When we look at this name of Jesus, we need to consider the setting. Philip finds Nathanael and tells him they have found the prophet Moses said was to come, as did the rest of the Old Testament prophets. In other words, "We have found the Messiah." Instead of debating about Jesus 'hometown, Philip simply says, "Come and see."

At this point, we take the liberty to imagine what Nathanael was thinking before the conversation that follows.

Jesus describes Nathanael (by the way, this is his known name, and his family name was Bartholomew. The other Gospels, when referring to Nathanael, use his family name, which means 'son of Tolmai' - Luke 6:14) as "a true Israelite in whom there is nothing false." Later, Jesus refers to angels ascending and descending on the Son of Man.

As we reflect on this, we believe there is a link back to the life and experiences of Jacob. Could it be that Nathanael was thinking about the deceit of Jacob as he sat under the fig tree? If he was, it helps us understand why Jesus would use this greeting and speak of angels ascending and descending. Jacob was full of deceit, and while the angels in Jacob's vision were going up and down on a ladder, there is no mention of a ladder in this conversation—because Jesus was the ladder.

"No one comes to the Father but by me" (John 14:6).

Jesus' Omniscience

Nathanael's question, "How do you know me?", reveals the nature of Jesus. John records in John 2:24-25, *"But Jesus on his part did not entrust himself to them, because he knew all people and needed no one to bear witness about man, for he himself knew what was in man."*

Jesus is omniscient—that is, all-knowing—which is an attribute of God. Psalm 139:1-18 gives insight into the Son of Man's omniscience. Let me quote part of that passage:

"O Lord, you have searched me and known me!

You know when I sit down and when I rise up; you discern my thoughts from afar.

You search out my path and my lying down and are acquainted with all my ways.

Even before a word is on my tongue, behold, O Lord, you know it altogether. You hem me in, behind and before, and lay your hand upon me.

Such knowledge is too wonderful for me; it is high; I cannot attain it."

Another example of Jesus' omniscience is found in John 4, in His conversation with the woman at the well. Jesus knew all about her life:

"Go, call your husband." "I have none."

"You are right. You have had five husbands, and the one you are living with is not your husband."

The Three Duties of Jesus, the Son of Man, in the Gospel of John

Now, let us examine the three duties of Jesus, the Son of Man, in the Gospel according to John.

The Son of Man as Judge

When we look at the Son of Man, we see that one day He will judge. He is qualified to judge because:

1. The Father gave Him that responsibility.
2. As the God-Man, He can represent humanity.
3. Being omniscient, nothing is hidden from Him.
4. Being holy, His judgment is righteous and just.

This is what underpins John 5:26-29:

"For as the Father has life in himself, so he has granted the Son also to have life in himself. And he has given him authority to execute judgment because he is the Son of Man. Do not marvel at this, for an hour is coming when all who are in the tombs will hear his voice and come out, those who have done good to the resurrection of life, and those who have done evil to the resurrection of judgment."

Here is the vital doctrine of the resurrection of the dead. As Jesus said:

"Do not be amazed at this; for an hour is coming in which all who are in their graves will hear His voice and come out." (John 5:28)

The Two Destinies After Death

When a person dies, there are only two destinies.

For the believer, it is to be "present with the Lord." Paul's words in 2 Corinthians 5:8 affirm this: *"Yes, we are of good courage, and we would rather be away from the body and at home with the Lord."* For the unbeliever, after death, the soul goes to Hades the prison for unbelieving spirits. This is clearly seen in Luke 16, in the account of the deaths of the rich man and Lazarus:

"The rich man also died and was buried, and in Hades, being in torment, he lifted up his eyes and saw Abraham far off and Lazarus at his side. And he called out, 'Father Abraham, have mercy on me, and send Lazarus to dip the end of his finger in water and cool my tongue, for I am in anguish in this flame.'….. between us and you a great chasm has been fixed, in order that those who would pass from here to you may not be able, and none may cross from there to us.'

And he said, 'Then I beg you, father, to send him to my father's house— for I have five brothers—so that he may warn them, lest they also come into this place of torment.' But Abraham said, 'They have Moses and the Prophets; let them hear them.'

And he said, 'No, Father Abraham, but if someone goes to them from the dead, they will repent.' He said to him, 'If they do not hear Moses and the Prophets, neither will they be convinced if someone should rise from the dead.'"

The Transition from Abraham's Side to Heaven

While Lazarus, the believer, went to Abraham's side, that location was only temporary because Jesus had not yet opened heaven's doors, so to speak, through His sacrifice on the cross.

Now, as Paul said in 2 Corinthians 5:8, when a believer dies, their body is folded up like a tent and placed in the ground, cremated, or cast into the sea, but their spirit is with the Lord.

However, the unbelieving dead will remain in Hades until the resurrection of the dead, when they will receive the sentence of their own choice—to be absent from the Lord forever and endure the judgment for their sin. Christ could have paid for their sin on their behalf, had they believed in Him.

Why Christ Came

This is why Christ came. He came as the Son of Man to save the lost. The fulfilment of this salvation will come at the second coming of Jesus.

The Second Duty of the Son of Man:

Atoning Sacrifice

The second duty of the Son of Man was to die as God's atoning sacrifice. Speaking to Nicodemus the chief religious' leader in Jerusalem, Jesus said,

"Just as Moses lifted up the serpent in the wilderness, even so must the Son of Man be lifted up, that everyone who believes in Him may have eternal life." (John 3:14-15)

Also, in John 8:28,

"So, Jesus said to them, 'When you have lifted up the Son of Man, then you will know that I am He...'"

The Lifting Up: A Prediction of His Crucifixion

The "lifting up" was Jesus predicting His crucifixion. His reference to Moses lifting up the serpent refers to Israel's rebellion during the 40 years of wandering in the wilderness. As judgment, God sent snakes that caused many people to die when bitten. This judgment brought repentance among the people.

But rather than removing the snakes, God provided a way to deal with the inescapable and certain death that could strike at any moment, as the snakes were everywhere. God instructed Moses to mould a bronze snake and place it on a pole where all could see. If they were bitten, all they had to do was look and they would live.

The consequence of the venom would be destroyed within their bodies through this irrational, illogical yet faith response to God's remedy: Look and you will live. This became a picture of Jesus power to save and His call to have faith in his redeeming sacrifice through the cross.

The Comparison to Jesus 'Death on the Cross

Think of it this way: they were asked to look at the snake, the very thing that had caused their imminent death. They were confronted with the consequence of their spiritual rebellion.

Jesus is drawing the comparison to His coming death on the cross. It was our sin that brought about the need for His death. As we have seen from the pending judgment in the first point, rebellion and unbelief face the wrath of God, as John 3:36 reminds us:

"Whoever believes in the Son has eternal life; whoever does not obey the Son shall not see life, but the wrath of God remains on him."

It is sin that has brought the wrath of God against us because *"all have sinned."* Romans 3:23

Jesus also teaches that salvation comes when God removes the death sentence by removing its cause—this is true for both venom and sin.

"As far as the east is from the west, so far does He remove our transgressions from us." (Psalm 103:12) *"God made Him who had no sin to be sin for us, so that in Him we might become the righteousness of God."* (2 Corinthians 5:21)

Salvation Through Faith.

The serpent on the pole and the trusting look highlights how salvation comes in both situations—their salvation from the snake bite and our salvation from sin. It comes through faith.

The look of faith was not just glancing around and seeing the snake on the pole. The look of faith meant personally believing what God had said through Moses and acting upon that belief.

The same is true for our salvation. Knowing about the biblical record of Jesus Christ will not save you. It requires trust and faith in all that Jesus has taught and done.

Understanding Saving Faith: John 6

Understanding what saving faith means is vital. Look at another Son of Man passage that also focuses on our salvation in John chapter 6.

After Jesus fed 5,000 people with five loaves and two small fish, He crossed Lake Galilee to Capernaum. The following day, He went into the synagogue and began to teach.

Those who had benefited from the free meal the previous day came looking for Jesus, hoping for another free meal. But Jesus wanted to take them beyond their physical needs and address their greater need for spiritual life.

"Do not work for the food that perishes, but for the food that endures to eternal life, which the Son of Man will give to you…" (John 6:27)

Jesus was saying that eternal life is a gift, "<u>Son of Man will give to you</u>" illustrating the grace of God. Jesus used the illustration of eating bread

- taking it into your body and receiving its benefits - to illustrate salvation's gracious offer. Just as you take bread into your body, one must bring Christ into their life to receive the benefits He brings; eternal life.

However, the people refused to understand and kept demanding that Jesus give them physical bread again.

This led the Son of Man to give a literal application: eat His flesh and drink His blood—a statement that was repulsive to the minds of His listeners.

"So Jesus said to them, 'Truly, truly, I say to you, unless you eat the flesh of the Son of Man and drink His blood, you have no life in you. Whoever feeds on My flesh and drinks My blood has eternal life, and I will raise him up on the last day. For My flesh is true food, and My blood is true drink. Whoever feeds on My flesh and drinks My blood abides in Me, and I in him. As the living Father sent Me, and I live because of the Father, so whoever feeds on Me, he also will live because of Me. This is the bread that came down from heaven, not like the bread the fathers ate, and died. Whoever feeds on this bread will live forever.'"

(John 6:53-58)

A Spiritual Meaning, Not Cannibalism

Do not misunderstand Jesus—He was not suggesting cannibalism. As He later explained to His disciples, His words were meant to be taken spiritually:

"The Spirit gives life; the flesh counts for nothing. The words I have spoken to you— they are full of the Spirit and life. Yet there are some of you who do not believe."
(John 6:63-64)

In other words, a person needs to bring the benefits of His flesh—that is, His life lived—and His blood— that is, His sacrifice—into their lives to receive eternal life.

Jesus explains it another way in John 17:3:

"This is eternal life: that they may know You, the only true God, and Jesus Christ, whom You have sent." The word "know" here refers to an intimate and personal relationship—not just intellectual knowledge or mere mental approval.

The Purpose of the Son of Man

This second reference to the Son of Man in John's Gospel can be best summarised with Mark 10:45: *"For even the Son of Man did not come to be served, but to serve, and to give His life as a ransom for many."*

The Third and Final Way the Title "Son of Man" Is Used in John:

His Glorification

God the Father Is Glorified in Him

"When he (Judas) had gone out, Jesus said, 'Now is the Son of Man glorified, and God is glorified in him. If God is glorified in him, God will also glorify him in himself and glorify him at once.'" John 13:31-32

God is glorified in the obedience of Christ, for He was going to be *"obedient unto death, even death on the cross."*

Remember that it was God who loved the world and sent His Son into the world. It was the Son who said: *"Here am I—it is written about me in the scroll—I have come to do your will, O God."* (Hebrews 10:7) It was God who *"laid on Him the iniquity of us all."* Isaiah 53:6.

Now, having returned to glory, Jesus receives the glory for the work He has finished.

He Is Glorified by Being Seated at God's Right Hand

John 17:5

"And now, Father, glorify me in your own presence with the glory that I had with you before the world existed."

When Jesus ascended into heaven, He was seated at the right hand of God the Father and became the object of worship.

"But when this priest (Jesus) had offered for all time one sacrifice for sins, he sat down at the right hand of God, and since that time he waits for his enemies to be made his footstool. For by one sacrifice, he has made perfect forever those who are being made holy." (Hebrews 10:12-14)

The fact that He sat down displayed that the work He was sent to earth to do was accomplished. His enthronement caused heaven to erupt into worship:

"Then I looked and heard the voice of many angels, numbering thousands upon thousands, and ten thousand times ten thousand. They encircled the throne and the living creatures and the elders. In a loud voice they were saying: Worthy is the Lamb, who was slain, to receive power and wealth and wisdom and strength and honour and glory and praise!

Then I heard every creature in heaven and on earth and under the earth and on the sea, and all that is in them, saying: 'To him who sits on the throne and to the Lamb be praise and honour and glory and power, for ever and ever!' The four living creatures said, 'Amen, 'and the elders fell down and worshiped." (Revelation 5:11-14)
This will fulfil the prayer of Jesus:

John 17:24

"Father, I want those you have given me to be with me where I am, and to see my glory, the glory you have given me because you loved me before the creation of the world."

His Glory Is Seen in His Authority. This was the promise of Psalm 110:1:

Identity

"The Lord says to my Lord: 'Sit at my right hand, until I make your enemies your footstool.'"

The Son of Man Is Given Dominion

Daniel 7:13-14

"I saw in the night visions, and behold, with the clouds of heaven there came one like a son of man, and he came to the Ancient of Days and was presented before him. And to him was given dominion and glory and a kingdom, that all peoples, nations, and languages should serve him; his dominion is an everlasting dominion, which shall not pass away, and his kingdom one that shall not be destroyed."

Ephesians 1:15-23 expands on this further:

"For this reason, because I have heard of your faith in the Lord Jesus and your love toward all the saints, I do not cease to give thanks for you, remembering you in my prayers, that the God of our Lord Jesus Christ, the Father of glory, may give you the Spirit of wisdom and of revelation in the knowledge of him, having the eyes of your hearts enlightened, that you may know.

1. What is the hope to which he has called you,

2. What are the riches of his glorious inheritance in the saints,

3. What is the immeasurable greatness of his power toward us who believe, according to the working of his great might that he worked in Christ when he raised him from the dead and seated him at his right hand in the heavenly places, Far above all rule and authority and power and dominion, and above every name that is named, not only in this age but also in the one to come. And he put all things under his feet and gave him as head over all things to (for the benefit of) the church, which is his body, the fullness of him who fills all in all."

The Cross: The Catalyst for Worship in Heaven

The Cross and what Jesus the Son of Man accomplished on it is the catalyst for much of the worship in heaven because through the Cross, there is an eternal harvest. Just before the Cross, Jesus made this statement:

John 12:23-24 *"The hour has come for the Son of Man to be glorified. Truly, truly, I say to you, unless a grain of wheat falls into the earth and dies, it remains alone; but if it dies, it bears much fruit."*

Jesus was that grain of wheat—He died, and now the fruit that glorifies Him is being harvested. We are the "much fruit." We are the people spoken of in Revelation 7:9-10:

"After this I looked, and there before me was a great multitude that no one could count, from every nation, tribe, people, and language, standing before the throne and before the Lamb. They were wearing white robes and were holding palm branches in their hands. And they cried out in a loud voice: 'Salvation belongs to our God, who sits on the throne, and to the Lamb!'"

Millions and millions of recipients of salvation— "all who believe in His Name"—will one day be resurrected and stand alive before Him, displaying His glorious grace. As Isaiah prophesied 800 years before Jesus' death:

Isaiah 53:11 *"He shall see of the travail of his soul and shall be satisfied."*

"He has blessed us in the Beloved. In him we have redemption through his blood, the forgiveness of our trespasses, according to the riches of his grace." His grace is glorious!

The Son of Man will be glorified, and our salvation will be one way that displays His glory.

Conclusion

Well, that brings us to the end of our discovery of who Jesus is in John chapter one.

Identity

Even after examining these 12 names of Jesus, the full story has not been told. However, now that we have gained this understanding of the lover of our souls, we will explore how Jesus made it possible to offer and secure our salvation. The answers can be found in John chapter two, where they are woven into two significant events in the life of Jesus."

Then, in chapters 3 to 11, we will see how John records Jesus' interactions with people and their responses.

Al Watson

Here are 10 questions based on our notes: Chapter 14

1. What is the significance of the title "Son of Man" in John's Gospel, and how does it connect to Daniel 7:13?

2. Jesus' omniscience is emphasised in the Gospel of John (e.g., His interaction with Nathanael and the woman at the well). How does this attribute support His role as Judge of mankind?

3. The study discusses how Jesus' crucifixion was prefigured by the bronze serpent in the wilderness (John 3:14-15). How does this Old Testament imagery deepen our understanding of salvation through Christ?

4. Jesus states in John 14:6, "No one comes to the Father but by me." How does this align with the concept of Jesus as the 'ladder' from Jacob's dream, as referenced in the study?

5. In John 6, Jesus uses the metaphor of eating His flesh and drinking His blood to illustrate salvation. How does this passage challenge common misunderstandings of faith and salvation?

6. The study emphasises two eternal destinies: being with the Lord or being separated from Him. How do passages like Luke 16 (the rich man and Lazarus) and 2 Corinthians 5:8 shape our understanding of life after death?

7. Jesus describes His glorification as being directly connected to His obedience, suffering, and resurrection (John 12:23-24). How does this challenge worldly views of glory and success?

8. John 5:26-29 presents Jesus as the ultimate Judge because of His divine authority and righteousness. How does this impact our understanding of accountability before God?

Identity

9. The study highlights that Jesus' atoning sacrifice was both necessary and sufficient for salvation (2 Corinthians 5:21). What are the implications of rejecting this sacrifice, according to John 3:36?

10. Revelation 5:11-14 and John 17:24 speak of Jesus' glorification in heaven. How does this final glorification fulfil the purpose of His mission on earth, and what does it mean for believers today.

Al Watson

Chapter Fifteen: The Wine and the Blood

John Chapter 2: The Real Reason for the Season

When Christmas rolls around, we often hear Christians say, "Jesus is the reason for the season," as an attempt to draw people's minds to the true reason for celebrating Christ's birth. This real reason is the question we seek to focus on in this chapter—John chapter 2.

As you will see, John takes two events and uses them to distil the real reason behind the saving work and power of Jesus Christ. But first, let's set the scene.

There is one word that is repeated three times, and each reference reveals a deeper insight into the message of the Gospel. It is the word *believe*. After turning water into wine, verse 11 states that His disciples "believed in Him".

Then, after referring to the destruction of the temple and being able to raise it up again in three days, the disciples realised this was referring to His resurrection. Verse 22 states, "they believed the Scriptures, and the word that Jesus had spoken".

The third instance is in response to the people seeing the miracles of Jesus. Verse 23 states, "many believed", but Jesus knew that it was a false belief. Obviously, there can be false faith.

We suggest this chapter is about the kind of believing that brings spiritual life to a Christ-follower and what it is that we need to believe in.

John starts with the timeline: "on the third day". Was this the third day of the week? Was it the third day after calling Nathanael? The answer is we really don't know.

John has already used some form of dating the events, because in chapter one, he refers to the next day in verses 29, 35, and 43. On day one, an interrogation group comes from Jerusalem to interview John the Baptist to determine if he was the promised Messiah. Then, on day two (verse 29), John the Baptist points to Jesus as the Messiah, God's Lamb who would take away the sins of the world.

On the third day, Jesus interacts with three potential followers: John, the writer of this Gospel, and Andrew and Peter. Then, on day four (verse 43), we have Jesus calling Philip, and then Philip finds Nathanael and brings him to Jesus. So, it would be fair to assume that the third day in chapter 2 refers to the following week.

On the third day, there was a wedding in Cana in Galilee. Jesus lived in Nazareth, so Cana was a six-kilometre walk heading north. When we read this narrative, it's easy to major on things that miss the main point. For example, the Jewish customs around weddings or the kind of wine Jesus miraculously made. We could focus on how Jesus, in this miracle, circumvented the natural process of grapes becoming wine. Viticulturists speak of bud burst, flowering, fruit set, berry development, and harvest. Then, it takes at least six months of maturing before anyone would want to consume the wine.

Nevertheless, Jesus is the Creator of all things, so circumventing the process involved in making wine was revealing His creative powers as the Son of God.

If John is directing our attention to what people are meant to believe, then we must take a closer look at the deeper significance of what is happening in his Gospel. Every event he records carries meaning beyond the surface. The elements within the narrative—such as the containers used in the miracle and the transformation of water into wine—are not merely incidental details but symbols that reveal

Identity

profound truths. The containers serve as vessels of revelation, while the wine itself points to a greater reality—one that is essential for a proper understanding of the Gospel message.

John himself provides us with a clear statement of his purpose in writing. His Gospel is not a random collection of events but a carefully chosen account designed to lead readers to faith. He explicitly tells us the reason for his writing, and it is through this lens that we should interpret his words. As he states:

"Now Jesus did many other signs in the presence of the disciples, which are not written in this book; but these are written so that you may believe that Jesus is the Christ, the Son of God, and that by believing you may have life in His name." (John 20:30–31)

This declaration frames everything within the Gospel, guiding us to see not only *what* happened but *why* it was recorded. The signs and miracles John includes are not merely demonstrations of power but carefully chosen testimonies, designed to draw people into belief in Jesus as the Christ, the Son of God, through whom eternal life is given.

We read that there were six stone water jars, each capable of holding between 20 to 30 gallons. If we take an average of 25 gallons per jar and multiply that by six, we arrive at a staggering total of 150 gallons—over 600 litres—of the finest quality wine ever made. But why such an abundant quantity? Surely, this detail is not included merely to impress us with the scale of the miracle. There is a deeper significance behind it.

John is not primarily drawing our attention to the miracle itself, which he refers to as a *sign*. His purpose is to direct our focus toward what this sign reveals. It is important to remember that when John was physically present at this wedding, witnessing the event unfold, he likely did not grasp the full significance of what had taken place. At that moment, he may have simply seen Jesus providing wine to save an embarrassed bridal couple from social disgrace. However, after the death and resurrection of Jesus, John, along with the other disciples, came to understand the true meaning behind these miraculous events. As Luke records in his Gospel, *"Then he opened their minds so they could understand the Scriptures"* (Luke 24:45). It was only in hindsight—some 25 to 30 years after the resurrection—that John, now with a deeper spiritual insight, wrote down these events with a clear understanding of the message Jesus intended to convey through them.

John refers to this miracle as the *first of his signs*, and the term *sign* is crucial because a sign always points to something beyond itself. The abundance of wine is not merely about restoring the dignity of a newlywed couple who underestimated their guests' consumption. If that were the sole purpose, Jesus could have simply instructed the servants to refill the empty wine-skins with water and then take a sample to the master of the feast. Instead, something far more significant is at work. It is even difficult to believe that a wedding party would have so drastically miscalculated their wine supply, suggesting that the deeper meaning of this event is what truly matters.

To uncover this meaning, we must first examine the six stone water jars mentioned in verse 6 and, more importantly, their intended use. These were not ordinary vessels; they were set apart for the Jewish rites of purification. This detail is significant because purification is at the heart of Jesus' mission. He came *to seek and to save the lost* (Luke 19:10), and He knew that lost people required cleansing—not just physical cleansing, but spiritual purification, a washing away of their sin. This theme of purification is central to the Gospel message, and John highlights it because his purpose in writing is to lay a strong foundation for understanding the transformative power of the Gospel.

This idea of purification is not new; it is a recurring theme throughout Scripture. The Old Testament, which John and his audience would have been deeply familiar with, contains numerous examples of God calling His people to be cleansed from sin. Isaiah proclaims this divine call:

"Wash yourselves; make yourselves clean; remove the evil of your deeds from before my eyes," says the Lord. "Come now, let us reason together," says the Lord. "Though your sins are like scarlet, they shall be white as snow; though they are red like crimson, they shall become like wool." (Isaiah 1:16-18)

King David, after being convicted of his own sin, pleaded with God for this very cleansing, praying:

"Wash me thoroughly from my iniquity, and cleanse me from my sin... Purge me with hyssop, and I shall be clean; wash me, and I shall be whiter than snow. Create in me a clean heart, O God, and renew a right spirit within me." (Psalm 51:2,7,10)

The theme of purification continues into the New Testament. The apostle Paul echoes this message when writing to the Corinthians, reminding them of the sinful lives they once lived:

"Do you not know that the unrighteous will not inherit the kingdom of God? Do not be deceived: neither the sexually immoral, nor idolaters, nor adulterers, nor men who practice homosexuality, nor thieves, nor the greedy, nor drunkards, nor revellers, nor swindlers will inherit the kingdom of God. <u>And such were some of you. But you were washed, you were sanctified, you were justified in the name of the Lord Jesus Christ and by the Spirit of our God.</u>" (1 Corinthians 6:9-11)

Paul's words make it clear: the Corinthian Christians had once lived according to the sinful culture around them, but through faith in the Gospel, they were washed, sanctified, and justified. Their cleansing was not a mere external ritual but an inward transformation accomplished *in the name of the Lord Jesus Christ and by the Spirit of our God.*

In the same way, John wants his readers to recognise that the miracle at Cana is not just about physical wine—it is a sign that points to the deeper reality of spiritual purification. The six stone jars, originally meant for ceremonial washing, are now repurposed in this miracle to illustrate a new kind of cleansing—one that goes beyond outward rituals and reaches the heart. Jesus is showing that He has come to provide the ultimate purification, not through water alone but through something far greater: the cleansing power of the sacrifice of Jesus on the cross, which leads to new life.

Where can we find this kind of personal spiritual cleansing today? A cleansing that, like David pleaded, can renew a right spirit within us? A cleansing so complete that it blots out all transgressions and brings transformation at the deepest level? A cleansing that not only washes away sin but changes the very desires that once controlled us, empowering us to live a new and fulfilling life?

John's message is clear: belief in the Gospel message offers this very cleansing. It is not just a doctrine or a theological concept—it is a reality that, once believed and embraced, brings total purification. This forgiveness, this renewal, this washing away of sin allows those who experience it to declare with confidence:

Once we were lost, *"but now we are washed. We have been sanctified, we have been justified in the name of the Lord Jesus Christ and by the Spirit of our God."* (1 Corinthians 6:11)

But this raises an important question: *How is such a cleansing possible?* How can sinful, broken people be washed and made pure? John directs us back to the six stone jars and their contents—wine. It is not the physical drink itself that holds significance, but what the wine *symbolises*.

Identity

To understand this symbolism, we must look to the final night of Jesus' life. On the eve of His crucifixion, He gathered with His disciples to celebrate the Jewish Passover—a festival that commemorated Israel's deliverance from slavery in Egypt. This was a time when the Israelites remembered how their ancestors were spared from God's judgment after they sacrificed a lamb and applied its blood to the doorposts of their homes. That night, the angel of death passed through Egypt, striking down the firstborn of every household—except those whose doors were marked with the blood of the sacrificial lamb. In those homes, judgment *passed over* them, sparing them from death. This is the origin of the Passover feast, a remembrance of God's deliverance.

It was during this sacred meal that Jesus introduced something new. He took two familiar symbols—a piece of unleavened bread and a cup of wine—and instituted what we now call *communion*. As He broke the bread, He declared, *"This is my body, given for you; do this in remembrance of me."* (Luke 22:19) At that moment, the disciples did not fully grasp what He meant. They did not yet understand that within hours, His body would be broken—beaten, pierced, and nailed to a cross.

Then Jesus took the cup—the cup of redemption in the Passover tradition—and made a profound declaration:

"This cup is the new covenant in my blood, which is poured out for you." (Luke 22:20)

But the cup did not contain blood; it contained *wine*. In this moment, wine became the symbol of His blood, the very blood He was about to shed. Jesus was proclaiming that His death—the sacrifice of His life—would establish a new covenant, a new way for humanity to be reconciled with God. Just as the blood of the lamb spared the Israelites from judgment, His blood would now provide the ultimate cleansing, allowing God's righteous judgement to *pass over* those who believe in Him. No longer would sin bring condemnation for those covered by His sacrifice. This is the source of true spiritual cleansing.

Through Christ's death, people can receive forgiveness—but this is not an abstract belief. It requires a faith that is deeply rooted in the truth of the Gospel, a faith that fully trusts in what Jesus has done. As John later wrote in his first epistle:

"The blood of Jesus Christ, God's Son, cleanses us from all sin." (1 John 1:7)

This is why believers partake in communion—not as a mere ritual, but as a sacred reminder of the cleansing power of Jesus' sacrifice. When we drink the wine, we remember that it is through His life given in our place when He shed His blood alone, that we are purified, forgiven, and made new. There is no other way to be cleansed from sin apart from the cross of Christ.

John's account of Jesus 'first miracle highlights two key truths. First, *"Through this, Jesus manifested His glory."* (John 2:11) In other words, this miracle was not just an act of kindness for a wedding couple; it was a revelation of who Jesus truly is and why He came into the world. Over time, people would come to understand that the transformation of water into wine was pointing to something far greater: the transformation of human lives through the cleansing power of His sacrifice. It is *His* blood, *His* life given for us, that brings about true purification.

Secondly, the sheer abundance of the wine in this miracle is no coincidence. Jesus did not merely provide enough to meet the immediate need—He created an overflowing supply. This abundance reveals His greater purpose: His sacrifice is not limited to a single group of people or a single moment in time. Instead, it extends to *all who will believe in Him.* Just as the wedding guests received more than enough, so too does the grace of God overflow beyond all measure, offering salvation and cleansing to anyone who places their faith in Jesus.

The first miracle recorded in John's Gospel is far more than an act of hospitality—it is a signpost pointing to the heart of the Gospel itself. Jesus, the true Passover Lamb, who came to bring the ultimate purification.

Through His sacrifice, the stain of sin can be washed away, lives can be transformed, and a new relationship with God can be made possible. And this offer stands open to all who will receive it.

Then, John confesses that because of this first miracle, *"the disciples believed in Him."* (John 2:11). This was a pivotal moment, marking a shift in the relationship between Jesus and His earliest followers. Up to this point, they had been observing, listening, and learning. But now, something had changed. Their understanding of who Jesus was deepened, and their faith in Him was confirmed in a new and profound way. As far as we know, there were five disciples present at this moment: John, Andrew, Peter, Philip, and Nathanael. These were the first men to follow Jesus, having encountered Him just a few weeks earlier. If we have the timeline correct, they had already spent some time interacting with Him, hearing Him teach, and witnessing His character. But this miracle at Cana—the first recorded sign—served as a turning point. It was no longer just about curiosity or intrigue; they now *believed* in Him. Their perspective shifted from seeing Him as merely a teacher or prophet to acknowledging Him as the Messiah, the One sent by God.

Although John's Gospel does not explicitly detail the content of Jesus' teachings up to this point, we can reasonably infer from the other Gospels that His message remained consistent. It is fair to assume that these five men had already heard Jesus explain how the Hebrew Scriptures foretold His coming, how He was fulfilling the promises of God, and how He was inviting people to become part of the Kingdom of God. John is making it clear: these five now understood that Jesus was not just another rabbi, nor even just a prophet.

He was the Messiah—*God's anointed Saviour of the world.*

This was the fulfilment of the promise God had made all the way back in the Garden of Eden. Jesus was the One who had come to *crush the head of the serpent* (Genesis 3:15), breaking the power of Satan and making it possible for people to be reconciled with God. This was not just about abstract theological truths—it was about real transformation. It was about restoring what had been lost through sin and opening the way for people to experience a new relationship with their Creator.

But John knows that Jesus 'message goes beyond cleansing, purification, and forgiveness. Yes, we need our sins forgiven, but the Gospel is about more than just wiping away our past—it is about stepping into a *new life*. The central question is not only *how can we be forgiven?* but also, *how can we now live in freedom from the ways of our past?*

This is where the message of Jesus is truly revolutionary. The Gospel is not simply about escaping judgment—it is about transformation. It is about living a *resurrected life*. When a person truly believes in Jesus, they are not merely *improved*; they are *made new*. This is the radical nature of Christianity: *lives can be completely changed*. The power of sin, addiction, and destructive patterns can be broken. No one is beyond redemption. There are no restrictions on who can receive this new life—no matter how dark or degrading one's past may have been, total transformation is possible.

This is the hope the Gospel offers: that in Christ, we are not only *forgiven*—we are *changed*.

To teach this second foundational truth of the Gospel, John takes an event that occurred in the final week of Jesus 'ministry—just before He went to the cross—and strategically places it at the *beginning* of his Gospel. Unlike the other Gospel writers, John does not follow a strict chronological order in his account of Jesus 'life. Instead, his Gospel is a *topical record*, structured not around timelines but around themes and spiritual truths. His primary aim is not merely to recount historical events but to *teach* what the Gospel is, so that people might believe in Jesus and receive eternal life. While Luke provides a carefully ordered timeline, John prioritises truth, arranging his material in a way that best reveals the message of salvation.

This explains why John brings forward an event from the last week of Jesus 'life and places it early in his Gospel narrative—Jesus' cleansing of the temple.

Identity

The event took place shortly after His triumphant entry into Jerusalem. Riding on a donkey, He had been welcomed by crowds shouting, *"Hosanna! Blessed is He who comes in the name of the Lord!"* (John 12:13). It was a moment of great public acclaim, yet Jesus did something unexpected upon entering the city: He went directly to the Temple. There, instead of embracing the religious leaders or offering a traditional teaching, He made a whip out of rope and forcefully drove out all those who were selling sacrificial animals. He commanded those selling doves to remove them immediately and then overturned the tables of the money changers, scattering their coins across the Temple courts.

At first glance, this act may seem shocking—especially from the One who is often portrayed as meek and gentle. But Jesus 'actions were not driven by uncontrolled anger; they were an expression of divine authority and righteous judgment. The Temple was meant to be a place of prayer, worship, and communion with God. Instead, it had been turned into a marketplace, a centre of greed and corruption. Worshippers who came with sincere hearts to offer sacrifices found themselves at the mercy of profiteering merchants. Those who brought money to give as an offering or to pay their religious taxes were told that their currency was "unclean" and had to be exchanged for "Temple money." But the exchange rates were heavily inflated, with large fees being taken by those in charge. What was meant to be an act of devotion had been turned into a business—an exploitation of the faithful. Jesus' dramatic cleansing of the Temple was a clear declaration that God's house was *not* to be desecrated by such corruption.

This bold act brought an immediate response from the Jewish religious leaders.

Their reaction is fascinating. They did not accuse Jesus of wrongdoing. They did not arrest Him on the spot. Instead, they demanded that He show them a *sign* to prove His authority. *"What sign do You show us for doing these things?"* they asked (John 2:18).

Their question reveals much about their hearts. They were not offended by the injustice that had taken place in the Temple. They were not concerned that their sacred space had been turned into a den of thieves. What troubled them was *Jesus Himself*—His authority, His challenge to their power, His disruption of their control. Rather than acknowledging their own corruption and repenting, they demanded proof that He had the right to expose their sin.

Yet, ironically, they already had more than enough proof. Just days before this event, Jesus had performed one of His most astonishing miracles—He had raised a man, Lazarus, from the dead after he had been in the tomb for *four days*. This was no secret; it was widely known among the people, and the religious leaders themselves had already held a council to discuss the implications of what Jesus had done. John records this meeting in John 11:47-53:

"So, the chief priests and the Pharisees gathered the council and said, 'What are we to do? For this man performs many signs. If we let him go on like this, everyone will believe in him, and the Romans will come and take away both our place and our nation.' But one of them, Caiaphas, who was high priest that year, said to them, 'You know nothing at all. Nor do you understand that it is better for you that one man should die for the people, not that the whole nation should perish.'"

John adds an important footnote to this conversation, revealing a deeper significance behind Caiaphas' words:

"He did not say this of his own accord, but being high priest that year, he prophesied that Jesus would die for the nation, and not for the nation only, but also to gather into one the children of God who are scattered abroad. So, from that day on they made plans to put Him to death." (John 11:51-53)

Here we see the real issue at hand. The religious leaders were not looking for *truth*—they were trying to *preserve their own power*. They feared that if too many people believed in Jesus, their control over the nation would slip away. They were willing to go to any lengths to prevent that from happening, even if it meant putting an innocent man to death. What Caiaphas spoke, thinking it was a political calculation, was in fact

Identity

a prophecy of divine purpose: Jesus *would* die, not just for Israel, but to bring salvation to all people who would believe in Him.

Thus, when the Jewish leaders later demanded a sign from Jesus, they were not genuinely seeking proof— they had already seen undeniable evidence of His power and authority. Their hearts were hardened, their motives self-serving. Their rejection of Jesus was not due to a lack of signs but to a refusal to surrender to the truth.

John places this event at the beginning of his Gospel to emphasis this second great truth of the Gospel: *Jesus came not only to cleanse individuals from sin but to confront the corruption of false religion and establish true worship.* His authority is not merely that of a wise teacher or a miracle worker—it is the authority of the very Son of God, the One who purifies not just the Temple, but the hearts of all who believe in Him.

If the religious leaders wanted a sign, Jesus would give them one. Like Caiaphas, He would offer a prophetic statement—one that would be fulfilled within days. He declared, *"Destroy this temple, and in three days I will raise it up."* (John 2:19).

The reaction was immediate. The Jewish leaders scoffed at His words, saying, *"It has taken forty-six years to build this temple, and will you raise it up in three days?"* (John 2:20). They assumed He was speaking about the physical structure that surrounded them—Herod's Temple, an architectural wonder of massive sandstone blocks, some weighing between 20 and 30 tons.

But Jesus was speaking of a far greater temple—the true centre of worship—*His own body*. John affirms this in hindsight, writing, *"But He was speaking about the temple of His body."* (John 2:21). This revelation forms the second half of the Gospel's message.

Al Watson

Question Time:

Here are 10 questions based on our notes: Chapter 15

1.
Why does John place such emphasis on the word "believe" in this chapter, and how do the three examples of belief (disciples, Scripture, false faith) challenge us personally?

2.
What is the deeper meaning behind Jesus turning water into wine at the wedding in Cana, especially concerning the theme of spiritual purification?

3.
Why is the abundance of wine in Jesus' first miracle significant beyond just meeting the needs of a wedding party?

4.
What do the six stone water jars used for Jewish purification rituals symbolise in the context of the Gospel message?

5.
How does understanding wine as a symbol of Jesus' blood during the Last Supper deepen our appreciation of the miracle at Cana?

6.
Why did Jesus cleanse the Temple, and what does this act reveal about the kind of worship and devotion God desires?

7.
What does Jesus' statement, "Destroy this temple, and in three days I will raise it up," teach us about His identity and mission?

8.
In what ways were the religious leaders more concerned about protecting their power than seeking the truth about Jesus?

Identity

9.

How does John use the order and structure of events in his Gospel (especially moving the temple cleansing to the beginning) to teach us the full meaning of the Gospel?

10.

Reflecting on John Chapter 2, how would you describe the *real reason* for Jesus' coming, based on both His first miracle and His confrontation at the Temple?

Al Watson

Identity

Chapter Sixteen: The Temple and the Resurrection

The radical nature of Christianity is: *lives can be completely changed*. The power of sin, addiction, and destructive patterns can be broken. No one is beyond redemption. There are no restrictions on who can receive this new life—no matter how dark or degrading one's past may have been, total transformation is possible.

This is the hope the Gospel offers: that in Christ, we are not only *forgiven*—we are *changed*.

To teach this second foundational truth of the Gospel, John takes an event that occurred in the final week of Jesus 'ministry—just before He went to the cross—and strategically places it at the *beginning* of his Gospel. Unlike the other Gospel writers, John does not follow a strict chronological order in his account of Jesus' life. Instead, his Gospel is a *topical record*, structured not around timelines but around themes and spiritual truths. His primary aim is not merely to recount historical events but to *teach* what the Gospel is, so that people might believe in Jesus and receive eternal life. While Luke provides a carefully ordered timeline, John prioritises truth, arranging his material in a way that best reveals the message of salvation.

This explains why John brings forward an event from the last week of Jesus' life and places it early in his Gospel narrative—Jesus' cleansing of the temple.

The event took place shortly after His triumphant entry into Jerusalem. Riding on a donkey, He had been welcomed by crowds shouting, *"Hosanna! Blessed is He who comes in the name of the Lord!"* (John 12:13). It was a moment of great public acclaim, yet Jesus did something unexpected upon entering the city: He went directly to the Temple. There, instead of embracing the religious leaders or offering a traditional teaching, He made a whip out of rope and forcefully drove out all those who were selling sacrificial animals. He commanded those selling doves to remove them immediately and then overturned the tables of the money changers, scattering their coins across the Temple courts.

At first glance, this act may seem shocking—especially from the One who is often portrayed as meek and gentle. But Jesus' actions were not driven by uncontrolled anger; they were an expression of divine authority and righteous judgment. The Temple was meant to be a place of prayer, worship, and communion with God. Instead, it had been turned into a marketplace, a centre of greed and corruption. Worshippers who came with sincere hearts to offer sacrifices found themselves at the mercy of profiteering merchants. Those who brought money to give as an offering or to pay their religious taxes were told that their currency was "unclean" and had to be exchanged for "Temple money." But the exchange rates were heavily inflated, with large fees being taken by those in charge. What was meant to be an act of devotion had been turned into a business—an exploitation of the faithful. Jesus' dramatic cleansing of the Temple was a clear declaration that God's house was *not* to be desecrated by such corruption.

This bold act brought an immediate response from the Jewish religious leaders.

Their reaction is fascinating. They did not accuse Jesus of wrongdoing. They did not arrest Him on the spot. Instead, they demanded that He show them a *sign* to prove His authority. *"What sign do You show us for doing these things?"* they asked (John 2:18).

Their question reveals much about their hearts. They were not offended by the injustice that had taken place in the Temple. They were not concerned that their sacred space had been turned into a den of thieves because they profited from it. What troubled them was *Jesus Himself*— His authority, His challenge to their power, His disruption of their control. Rather than acknowledging their own corruption and repenting, they demanded proof that He had the right to expose their sin.

Yet, ironically, they already had more than enough proof. Just days before this event, Jesus had performed one of His most astonishing miracles—He had raised a man, Lazarus, from the dead after he had been in the tomb for *four days*. This was no secret; it was widely known among the people, and the religious leaders themselves had already held a council to discuss the implications of what Jesus had done. John records this meeting in John 11:47-53:

"So, the chief priests and the Pharisees gathered the council and said, 'What are we to do? For this man performs many signs. If we let him go on like this, everyone will believe in him, and the Romans will come and take away both our place and our nation.' But one of them, Caiaphas, who was high priest that year, said to them, 'You know nothing at all. Nor do you understand that it is better for you that one man should die for the people, not that the whole nation should perish.'"

John adds an important footnote to this conversation, revealing a deeper significance behind Caiaphas' words:

"He did not say this of his own accord, but being high priest that year, he prophesied that Jesus would die for the nation, and not for the nation only, but also to gather into one the children of God who are scattered abroad. So, from that day on they made plans to put Him to death." (John 11:51-53)

Here we see the real issue at hand. The religious leaders were not looking for *truth*—they were trying to *preserve their own power*. They feared that if too many people believed in Jesus, their control over the nation would slip away. They were willing to go to any lengths to prevent that from happening, even if it meant putting an innocent man to death. What Caiaphas spoke, thinking it was a political calculation, was in fact a prophecy of divine purpose: Jesus *would* die, not just for Israel, but to bring salvation to all people who would believe in Him.

Thus, when the Jewish leaders later demanded a sign from Jesus, they were not genuinely seeking proof— they had already seen undeniable evidence of His power and authority. Their hearts were hardened, their motives self-serving. Their rejection of Jesus was not due to a lack of signs but to a refusal to surrender to the truth.

John places this event at the beginning of his Gospel to emphasis this second great truth of the Gospel: *Jesus came not only to cleanse individuals from sin but to confront the corruption of false religion and establish true worship.* His authority is not merely that of a wise teacher or a miracle worker— it is the authority of the very Son of God, the One who purifies not just the Temple, but the hearts of all who believe in Him.

If the religious leaders wanted a sign, Jesus would give them one. Like Caiaphas, He would offer a prophetic statement—one that would be fulfilled within days. He declared, *"Destroy this temple, and in three days I will raise it up."* (John 2:19).

The reaction was immediate. The Jewish leaders scoffed at His words, saying, *"It has taken forty-six years to build this temple, and will you raise it up in three days?"* (John 2:20). They assumed He was speaking about the physical structure that surrounded them—Herod's Temple, an architectural wonder of massive sandstone blocks, some weighing between 20 and 30 tons.

But Jesus was speaking of a far greater temple—the true centre of worship—*His own body*. John affirms this in hindsight, writing, *"But He was speaking about the temple of His body."* (John 2:21). This revelation forms the second half of the Gospel's message.

The first truth of the Gospel is the *cross*—the cleansing power of Christ's sacrifice, symbolised by the wine at Cana. But forgiveness alone is not enough; we need more than cleansing. The second truth of the Gospel is *resurrection power*—the ability to overcome the corruption within us and live a transformed life.

Jesus was not just talking about the destruction and rebuilding of a building; He was speaking of His own death and resurrection, through which He would make it possible for *us* to be made new.

Just as His body would be broken and raised again, so too must *our* old way of life be put to death so that we may receive a new life. The Bible teaches that when we come to Christ, our bodies become the *temple of the Holy Spirit*, and it is His presence in us that brings the power to live righteously. The Christian life is not simply about having our sins forgiven—it is about living in the power of Christ's resurrection. Peter put it this way:

"He himself bore our sins in his body on the tree, that we might die to sin and live to righteousness." (1 Peter 2:24)

Paul echoes this in Philippians 3:10, stating his goal:

"That I may know Him and the power of His resurrection."

And in Romans 8:4, he adds:

"In order that the righteous requirement of the law might be fulfilled in us, who walk not according to the flesh but according to the Spirit."

This is where the power of the Gospel becomes personal. Before coming to Christ, we were powerless to live a truly righteous life. Even after believing in Him, if left to our own strength, we still cannot overcome the sinful desires that once controlled us. We need an *external* source of power—one that is greater than our old nature.

Paul understood this truth well. The key to victory, he explains, is that we *must not live according to the flesh but according to the Spirit*. After His resurrection, Jesus ascended to the Father, and ten days later, on the Day of Pentecost, He sent the Holy Spirit to empower His followers. It is the Spirit of God dwelling within believers that makes the Christian life possible.

Paul describes this transformation in Galatians 2:20:

"I have been crucified with Christ. It is no longer I who live, but Christ who lives in me. And the life I now live in the flesh I live by faith in the Son of God, who loved me and gave Himself for me."

What Does This Look Like in Practical Terms?

How does this transformation take place in real life? It begins with a conscious decision—a decision to *become a slave*.

Throughout the New Testament, we often see believers referring to themselves as *servants* of Christ.

However, the word *servant* does not fully capture the meaning of the original Greek word used in these passages. The word they used was *doulos*, which does not mean *servant* in the way we might think of today—it means *slave*.

Understandably, modern translators have often softened this term due to the historical weight the word *slave* carries. However, in the time of the New Testament, *doulos* referred to someone who was *completely given over to the will of another*. W.E. Vine's *Expository Dictionary of New Testament Words* defines *doulos* as: *"From deo, to bind, a slave, originally the lowest term in the scale of servitude, came also to mean one who gives himself up to the will of another."*

This is what it means to be a Christian. It is not merely about believing intellectually in Christ—it is about surrendering our entire will to Him. To be a Christian is to *give oneself completely* to the will of Jesus Christ.

When we do this, our lives will naturally begin to reflect *His* values, *His* responses, *His* actions, and *His* words. In other words, we will begin to live a righteous, holy, Christ-like life—not by our own effort, but by the power of the Holy Spirit working in us.

Paul describes this process beautifully in Philippians 2:13:

"For it is God who works in you, both to will and to work for His good pleasure."

This is the heart of the Christian life: *God Himself works within us, shaping our desires, renewing our will, and empowering us to live in a way that pleases Him.*

The Gospel's Complete Picture

John presents the full message of the Gospel through these two powerful symbols:

The Cross – Cleansing Through Christ's Blood

- Symbolising the blood of Christ is the wine at Cana. The water was for purification, but only the blood of Christ cleanses.
- It represents the forgiveness of sins through Jesus' sacrifice.

The Resurrection – Empowerment Through the Holy Spirit

- The resurrection of Jesus came after His body was destroyed, but through it, He destroyed sin and death. He is now the meeting place between God and man—it is no longer a temple.
- The power that raised Christ is the power that transforms our lives through the indwelling Holy Spirit, making us the temple of the Living God.

We need both. Forgiveness alone is not enough—we also need the *power* to live a new life. This power does not come from human effort but from surrendering ourselves fully to Christ and allowing the Holy Spirit to work in us.

John's Gospel is not just telling us about Jesus—it is *calling us to a decision*. Will we simply admire Him from a distance, or will we truly give ourselves over to Him as *doulos*—as slaves of Christ, living not by our own strength but by the power of His Spirit?

This is the invitation of the Gospel: not just to be cleansed, but to be *changed*.

The religious leaders would indeed destroy the temple of Jesus—*His body*—but, just as He prophesied, after three days, He would rise from the dead, and a *new* temple would be established.

For centuries, the Temple in Jerusalem had been the sacred meeting place between God and His people. It was there that sacrifices were offered, prayers were made, and atonement for sin was sought. But now, something new was happening. No longer would a physical building be the place where humanity encountered God. Instead, *Jesus Himself* would be the true temple—the place where God and man meet. Jesus made this clear when He later declared:

"I am the Way, the Truth, and the Life. No one comes to the Father except through Me." (John 14:6)

Most Jewish people knew their Scriptures well, for they were read to them at length every Sabbath with their local Synagogues. As they reflected on Jesus' words and actions, they would have recalled the promises God had made through the prophet Ezekiel:

"I will sprinkle clean water on you, and you shall be clean from all your uncleannesses, and from all your idols I will cleanse you. And I will give you a new heart, and a new spirit I will put within you. And I will remove the heart of stone from your flesh and give you a heart of flesh. And I will put My Spirit within you, and cause you to walk in My statutes and be careful to obey My rules." (Ezekiel 36:25-27)

This is precisely what Jesus' death and resurrection would accomplish.

Now, for the first time, the disciples *fully* believed. Because their faith was in Jesus—it was now also in *the Scriptures*. John emphasises this point:

"When therefore He was raised from the dead, His disciples remembered that He had said this, and they believed the Scripture and the word that Jesus had spoken." (John 2:22)

This tells us something profound about faith. True belief in Jesus is not just an emotional response, nor is it based on religious tradition. It is rooted in the *Word of God*. Faith comes by hearing, and hearing the Word of Christ. (Romans 10:17.)

True Faith is Based on Scripture

To believe in Jesus means to *believe in the Scriptures*. It is not about following religious customs, human traditions, or the teachings of spiritual leaders. It is not about redefining faith to suit personal preferences. True faith is anchored in *what God has revealed* through His Word.

John was not writing his Gospel in isolation. By the time he penned these words, the Church had already spread throughout the Roman world. This was the last of the four Gospels to be written, likely in the final decade of the first century, though some scholars place it in the early second century.

Why does this matter? Because by this time, Christ-followers already understood that Jesus was the *fulfilment* of the key Old Testament festivals. Paul makes this explicit when he writes:

"For Christ, our Passover Lamb, has been sacrificed." (1 Corinthians 5:7)

Paul also links this to the Festival of Unleavened Bread, which immediately followed Passover: *"Cleanse out the old leaven that you may be a new lump, as you really are unleavened. For Christ, our Passover Lamb, has been sacrificed."*

The Symbolism of the Passover and Unleavened Bread

In preparation for Passover, every Jewish household would undergo a *meticulous* cleaning to remove all traces of leaven (yeast) from their homes. According to the Law, *any* leaven in the house would disqualify them from participating in the festival. This was not merely a physical act—it was deeply symbolic.

Leaven represented *sin*. The removal of leaven from the home was a vivid reminder that God's true Passover Lamb—Jesus—would one day remove *sin* from the lives of those who believe in Him.

Jesus fulfilled this prophecy on the Cross. His death provided the ultimate cleansing, removing the sin that separated humanity from God. The Feast of Unleavened Bread lasted for seven days after Passover, reinforcing the idea that those who had been redeemed were now called to live lives free from sin.

Jesus Cleansing the Temple: The Spiritual Leaven

Now we see the link between Jesus cleansing the Temple and the Old Testament festivals.

As a twelve-year-old boy, Jesus had referred to the Temple as *"My Father's house"* (Luke 2:49). Now, as an adult, He returned—not just to *visit*, but to *cleanse* it. In doing so, He was removing the *leaven* of greed and corruption from His Father's house.

But this cleansing pointed to something far greater. Soon, Jesus Himself would become the *true* Passover Lamb. Just as the Jewish people slaughtered lambs to commemorate their deliverance from Egypt, Jesus would be crucified as the ultimate sacrifice for sin—on the very day the Passover lambs were being killed. John tells us that after the resurrection, the disciples *finally* understood the significance of these events: They now saw how the entire history of Israel—*the Passover, the Feast of Unleavened Bread, and even the Temple itself*—all pointed to Jesus. His death brought *cleansing*, His burial removed *sin*, and His resurrection *conquered* sin, death, and the power of the enemy.

Because Jesus was the first to rise from the dead, never to die again, He is called the *firstfruits* of those who will follow (1 Corinthians 15:20). The feast of firstfruits was always on the first Sunday after Passover, you can check this out in Leviticus 23. If you look at it carefully, it will cause you to question the notion that Jesus was crucified on Friday. Look for the special Sabbath day (John 19:31) and work back from the only specified day in the week Sunday, knowing that Jesus said He would be in the grave for three days and three nights. Mark 8:31, 9:31, 10:34 . Also remember that the Jewish day starts at 6pm each night. This goes back to creation where the evening came first then daylight- evening and morning. Genesis 1:5, 8,13,19,23.

The Warning of False Faith

John concludes this chapter with a sobering insight:

"Now when He was in Jerusalem at the Passover Feast, many believed in His name when they saw the signs that He was doing. But Jesus, on His part, did not entrust

Himself to them, because He knew all people and needed no one to bear witness about man, for He Himself knew what was in man." (John 2:23-25)

Many *believed*—but Jesus did not *entrust* Himself to them. Why? Because their faith was not *genuine*. It was a superficial faith—based on miracles, signs, and wonders, rather than on, as the Apostle Paul summarised his message to the Elders of the Ephesian Church in Acts 20, *"how I did not shrink from declaring to you anything that was profitable, and teaching you in public and from house to house, testifying both to Jews and to Greeks of <u>repentance toward God and of faith in our Lord Jesus Christ.</u>"* v20-21.

This raises an uncomfortable question:

Were these the same people who, just a few days later, would shout, *"Crucify Him!"*?

It is a sobering reality that many claim to have faith in Jesus, yet their belief is not *true saving faith*. True faith is not merely believing in miracles, nor is it about following religious tradition. It is about surrendering fully to Christ—giving up one's own will to embrace *His*.

John has shown us in this chapter that true faith involves:

- Believing in Jesus as the Messiah, the Son of God.
- Trusting in His sacrifice on the Cross and the Resurrection to deal with your sin issue.
- Believing in the Scriptures, not human tradition.
- Surrendering to Jesus as Lord, living not for self, but for Him.

Anything less is not the faith that brings people out of darkness and into the Kingdom of God.

Colossians 1:13,14 *"He has delivered us from the domain of darkness and transferred us to the kingdom of his beloved Son, in whom we have redemption, the forgiveness of sins."*

Identity

In the next book in the John Series, "ENCOUNTERS", we will follow John as he reveals how Jesus interacted with people from all walks of life, exposing their real spiritual problems and providing the answers they needed. Our hope is that by examining these interactions, we will embrace some of these insights as we seek to introduce people to the Saviour of the World.

Al Watson

Here are 10 questions based on our notes: Chapter 16

1. Why is forgiveness alone not enough in the Christian life, according to the teaching of the cross and resurrection?

2. What does it mean for the believer's body to become the "temple of the Holy Spirit," and how does this relate to living a transformed life?

3. Explain how the Christian life is more than having sins forgiven. What role does the resurrection power of Christ play in daily living?

4. Paul speaks about walking "not according to the flesh but according to the Spirit" (Romans 8:4). What does living by the Spirit look like practically in your own life?

5. The lecture mentions the Greek word *doulos* meaning "slave." How does understanding yourself as a "slave of Christ" challenge or change your view of Christian discipleship?

6. John connects the Gospel symbols of the Cross and Resurrection to the Festivals of Passover and Unleavened Bread, and Feast of Firstfruits. How do these Old Testament festivals deepen our understanding of Jesus' work?

7. How does Jesus' cleansing of the Temple reflect the deeper spiritual cleansing He wants to bring into our lives?

8. What does it mean that Jesus Himself is now the meeting place between God and man, and not a physical temple?

9. John highlights the danger of "false faith" based on signs and wonders. How can we examine our own faith to ensure it is rooted in true belief and surrender?

10. True faith involves believing in Jesus, trusting Scripture, and surrendering to His Lordship. Which of these areas do you find most challenging, and how can you grow in it?

Al Watson

www.ingramcontent.com/pod-product-compliance
Lightning Source LLC
Chambersburg PA
CBHW050338010526
44119CB00049B/600